To STE

ENJOY YOUR STUDY!!
xxx
"

HAPPY 61ST BIRTHDAY"

The Complete Guide to Rhodesian Ridgebacks

Tarah Schwartz

Publication Data

Tarah Schwartz

The Complete Guide to Rhodesian Ridgebacks ---- First edition.

Summary: "Successfully raising a Rhodesian Ridgeback dog from puppy to old age" --- Provided by publisher.

ISBN: 978-1-68960-6-783

[1. Rhodesian Ridgebacks --- Non-Fiction] I. Title.

This book has been written with the published intent to provide accurate and author-itative information in regard to the subject matter included. While every reasonable pre-caution has been taken in preparation of this book the author and publisher expressly dis-claim responsibility for any errors, omissions, or adverse effects arising from the use or application of the information contained inside. The techniques and suggestions are to be used at the reader's discretion and are not to be considered a substitute for professional veterinary care. If you suspect a medical problem with your dog, consult your veterinarian.

Design by Sorin Rădulescu

First paperback edition, 2019

TABLE OF CONTENTS

CHAPTER 1
The Rhodesian Ridgeback

What Is a Rhodesian Ridgeback?

The Rhodesian Ridgeback is an athletic, dignified hound whose signature characteristic is a ridge of backward-facing hair along the spine. The breed was originally developed in Africa for the purpose of tracking and baying lions. Although they are no longer used to hunt lions, they are competitive participants in a variety of modern dog sports. They also make great companions for active families, provided they are willing to deal with the Ridgeback's independent nature and high prey drive.

Rhodesian Ridgebacks are known for their calm and gentle demeanor, and many get along well with children and other pets. However, they are large, energetic dogs and must be monitored closely to ensure they don't play

Photo Courtesy of Liesl Kruger

too roughly with smaller play-mates. They are brave and loy-al dogs who may become shy or aggressive around strang-ers if not socialized properly. Rhodesian Ridgebacks are in-telligent and capable of learn-ing quickly, but their indepen-dence may present a challenge during training. Firm and con-sistent training methods work best with this breed. They are incredibly athletic dogs who require plenty of daily exer-cise. Without enough exercise, they may become high-strung or destructive.

Photo Courtesy of
Ash Watts

The coat of the Rhodesian Ridgeback is short, smooth, and easy to care for. Coat colors may range from light wheaten to deep-er browns and shades of red. Small patches of white may be found on the dog's chest or toes. There is a characteristic symmetrical stripe of hairs growing in the opposite direction along the dog's back. The coat requires relatively little grooming, but Rhodesian Ridgebacks are considered to be average shedders.

Rhodesian Ridgebacks' natural athleticism make them a popular choice for dog sport competitors. In addition to conformation and obedience, Ridgebacks excel in agility, dock diving, tracking, and lure coursing. The breed can be stubborn, but with firm and consistent training, they can be taught any number of commands. They also make excellent jogging com-panions and will gladly accompany their families on camping and hiking trips of any length.

Rhodesian Ridgebacks are considered to be relatively healthy dogs, but there are a few genetic issues that affect the breed. Hip and elbow dyspla-sia are common afflictions, but can be prevented with responsible testing and breeding practices. Thyroid disease affects nearly one in four Ridge-backs. Cataracts and heart disease are also common in the breed. As large, deep-chested dogs, they are prone to bloat, which is when a dog's stomach fills with gas, and can be fatal if not treated immediately. Overall, the breed is quite healthy and the average lifespan is around 10 to 12 years.

History of the Rhodesian Ridgeback

FUN FACT

Renaissance Hound

Originally traced to Africa, Rhodesian Ridgebacks were bred to track and bay at lions. This breed has a strong prey drive and is protective, fast, and powerful. Reaching up to 85 pounds, the Ridgeback is not a breed for first-time dog owners. It comes in at 42nd in the American Kennel Club's (akc.org) favorite breeds.

The Rhodesian Ridgeback was originally developed in southern Africa. Native to Rhodesia, now known as Zimbabwe, the breed was created by crossing the ridgebacked dogs kept by local tribes with the dogs kept by Boer settlers in the 16th and 17th centuries. European settlers quickly recognized the dog's innate talent for hunting and the breed became a popular choice for hunters in Matabeleland and Mashonaland. Hunters then began adding European breeds such as Pointers, Lurchers, Terriers, and Bulldogs to the mix in an attempt to create the perfect hunting dog. The Great Dane was even added into the bloodline in some areas, contributing size and a more muscular build. It is suspected that other Mastiff-type breeds were also added, but there is no official record of it.

The exact shape and size of the dogs varied by region, so a breed standard was proposed in 1925 by Francis Richard Barnes. Barnes was a well-known Ridgeback breeder of the time, who used the Dalmatian's breed standard as a starting point. The Rhodesian Lion Dog, as Barnes referred to the breed, was accepted by the South African Kennel Union in 1927, at which point the name was changed to Rhodesian Ridgeback. As the breed became more consistent and more popular with lion hunters, interest abroad began to grow. Rhodesian Ridgebacks were first imported into the United States in 1950 by William H. O'Brien and his wife. Mr. and Mrs. O'Brien imported six Rhodesian Ridgebacks with the intention of getting the breed recognized by the American Kennel Club. The breed and its official standard were eventually accepted by the AKC in 1955. In the United Kingdom, the Rhodesian Ridgeback Club of Great Britain was founded in 1952 in order to promote the breed among English dog fanciers.

Today, the breed has grown in popularity and the AKC currently ranks it in popularity as number 41 out of 193 recognized breeds. Although no longer used for hunting lions, Rhodesian Ridgebacks are often still used to hunt smaller game. They are successful competitors in lure coursing, conformation, and tracking competitions. Rhodesian Ridgebacks are also popular as family companions and exercise partners.

Photo Courtesy of Stephanie Egger

Physical Characteristics

Photo Courtesy of Charlene Walsh

Rhodesian Ridgebacks are large dogs that are slightly longer than they are tall, but with a balanced appearance. Males typically measure 25 to 27 inches in height at the shoulder and females measure 24 to 26 inches. The average weight is 70 to 85 pounds. The overall appearance of the dog should be that of a strong and muscular hound. They are active, athletic dogs and their build should reflect this.

The head of the Rhodesian Ridgeback is broad, with a long and powerful muzzle. Eyes should be round, bright, and of a color that complements the coat of the dog. Dogs with black noses should have darker eyes, while dogs with liver or brown noses are permitted to have amber-colored eyes. Darker coloring on the face and muzzle is acceptable within the guidelines of the breed standard. The nose should be black, brown, or liver in color. The Rhodesian Ridgeback's neck should appear fairly long and balanced. The chest should be deep, but not too wide or rounded. The shoulders are muscular, and the forelegs are straight and heavy in bone. The dog's feet are compact and rounded. Dewclaws may be present, or they may be removed. The Ridgeback's hindquarters are strong, muscular, and straight when viewed from behind.

The Rhodesian Ridgeback's coat should be short, dense, and glossy. The color may vary from a light shade of wheaten to a more reddish wheaten color. A small amount of white is allowed on the toes and chest, but excessive white, or white on any other part of the body, is undesirable. The characteristic feature of the Rhodesian Ridgeback is the ridge of hair growing in the opposite direction along the dog's spine. The ridge should be well-defined and symmetrical. Ideally, it should start just behind the shoulders and continue to the hips. The ridge should also contain two crowns, or whorls, directly opposite each other. In the show ring, a dog with only one crown, or more than two, will be seriously faulted. A dog with no ridge at all will be disqualified.

The gait of the Rhodesian Ridgeback should appear balanced and free, reflecting the breed's athleticism and endurance. The dog's stride should be long and efficient. Overall, the dog's movement should display an ideal balance between power and elegance.

Breed Behavioral Characteristics

Despite their history as fierce hunters, Rhodesian Ridgebacks are calm and gentle when at home with family. They are typically good-natured, obedient dogs who do well with children. Some Ridgebacks, especially young puppies, may play roughly and accidentally knock over small children or other pets, but it is purely by accident rather than malice. They are incredibly loyal dogs and can be somewhat reserved around strangers, so proper socialization is a necessity. In training, they are intelligent and learn quickly, but they can easily sense when they have the upper hand. They require confident, consistent trainers who regularly remind the dog of his place in the pack. Without firm leadership, Ridgebacks can become unmanageable and destructive. They are a high-energy breed who need regular physical and mental stimulation. They can be somewhat stubborn, especially if they believe that they are the leaders of the pack. The breed typically gets along well with animals of other species, provided they are socialized properly. Rhodesian Ridgebacks are active, athletic dogs who enjoy physical activity, especially alongside members of their family.

Photo Courtesy of Channing Mae Malz

Is a Rhodesian Ridgeback the Right Fit for You?

Rhodesian Ridgebacks are lively, energetic dogs that require a lot of physical and mental stimulation. You need to be honest with yourself about whether or not this is the right type of dog for you. If you are a person who enjoys spending your days off relaxing at home in front of the television, you may want to rethink adopting a Ridgeback. On the other hand, if you are an active person who spends your free time hiking, running, or exploring the outdoors, your lifestyle may be more ideal for the breed. This is not to say that Ridgebacks don't enjoy down time, as they do enjoy relaxing with their families, but they also need a significant amount of exercise. A tired dog will always be less likely to get into trouble than a dog who hasn't received enough stimulation.

Rhodesian Ridgebacks are likely to find ways to entertain themselves if you don't do it for them. If you work long hours and expect your dog to rest quietly all day while you're away, this breed may not be right for you. If given enough physical and mental stimulation, a Ridgeback will happily rest all

Photo Courtesy of
Rebecca Weddell

day until you return, but a bored Ridgeback can be quite destructive and will happily entertain herself in your absence by shredding throw pillows, getting into the trash, chewing on furniture, and generally turning your home into a disaster area. Exercising and keeping a Rhodesian Ridgeback busy can be a big time commitment, so if you don't have a lot of spare time you may want to consider another breed or type of pet.

Size could be a consideration, depending on your home. If you live in the country with no shortage of space, you may not need to worry about what size dog you bring home. However, if you live in a tiny apartment, you may need to consider whether that environment is right for a Rhodesian Ridgeback. Ridgebacks can make excellent apartment dogs provided they get enough physical and mental exercise. However, you need to consider how easy it would be to share such a cramped space with a large dog. You'll need to determine if you have enough room in the apartment for a crate or dog bed. If you choose to allow your dog on the furniture, consider whether there will still be enough room for you and your significant other or friends. If properly trained and exercised, it can be relatively easy to live with a large dog in a small space, but it will take time for you both to adapt to living in tight quarters and you need to seriously consider whether this is something you're willing to do.

You may also want to consider the Rhodesian Ridgeback's coat type if you live in a cold climate. Ridgebacks were developed in southern Africa and are incredibly heat tolerant dogs. Their short coats are ideal for protecting them against sun but still keeping them relatively cool. In a cold climate, however, their sleek coats may not be enough to keep them warm. Many Ridgebacks do well in frigid temperatures if they are dressed in coats, sweaters, or boots, but they still may not be able to spend much time outdoors without getting cold. If you live in an area with long, harsh winters, you may want to consider a breed which is more adapted to your climate.

CHAPTER 2
Choosing a Rhodesian Ridgeback

Buying vs. Adopting

Now that you've made the decision to bring a Rhodesian Ridgeback into your home, you need to decide whether you want to buy your new dog from a reputable breeder or adopt one from a shelter or rescue organization. Consider the ideal traits you are looking for in your new dog such as age, gender, level of training, and athletic potential. Knowing what you want from your new dog will not only help you decide where to look, but it will also help you in choosing which dog to bring home.

Photo Courtesy of
Michelle Gasaway

Photo Courtesy of
Sandy Gilbert

When deciding where to look for your new Ridgeback, think about whether you would prefer a puppy or an adult dog. Puppies are a lot of work and require constant supervision and training, but you have the advantage of being able to teach them the way you want. Adult dogs are often already housetrained, and they usually understand the basic rules of living in a house. However, sometimes they have developed bad habits in previous homes that you will need to work on to eliminate. Shelters are a great place to find older dogs, but they often have puppies as well. Some breeders may also have adult dogs available for adoption, usually retired show or breeding dogs.

Many dog owners do not have a preference on their new dog's gender, but some do, especially if they have other dogs at home. It's not uncommon for some female dogs to have a difficult time getting along with other female dogs, and some male dogs may prefer the company of a certain gender, so if you have a particularly opinionated dog at home, consider his or her preferences when deciding on a new dog. Many dogs will just be happy to have a new playmate, so they may not care what gender the new dog is, and you'll need the make the decision yourself.

If you have certain goals in mind for your new dog, you'll need to keep these in mind during your search. If you're looking for a companion dog with a heart of gold, you'll have equal chances of finding your dream dog with a breeder or with a rescue organization. However, if you're looking for a dog with perfect conformation who will do well in the show ring, you probably won't find what you're looking for at a shelter. Depending on your needs, you may want to look into breeders and rescue organizations to make sure you've considered all options in your search for the perfect dog.

How to Find a Reputable Breeder

If you've decided to get your puppy from a breeder, make sure you do your homework and choose a reputable breeder. You should carefully research a breeder before making any decisions and not impulsively purchase the first Ridgeback puppy you find. Reputable breeders are passionate about the breed and work hard to improve the health and well-being of the breed as a whole. Breeders who test their dogs for genetic conditions and show or compete with their dogs will give you the best chance at finding a healthy puppy that can do what you require. They will have records of the parent dogs and will be able to tell you about their temperaments, personalities, and accomplishments in the show ring.

One of the best ways to find a reputable breeder is by contacting other Rhodesian Ridgeback owners, especially if you intend to show your new dog. If you have a particular sport in mind, attend a few competitions or practices and talk to other Ridgeback handlers. You'll be able to see what kind of dogs certain breeders are producing and can decide whether they are breeding the type of dog you're looking for. Competitors will be able share their own experiences with local breeders and help you make an informed decision on where to get your new dog.

You can also search for breeders on the internet, but as with everything online, it's important to be cautious. Do your research and make sure the breeder is who they say they are, and their dogs are of the quality they're advertised to be. Many breeders keep websites that are up to date with their dogs' latest health tests and performance records. They may also have available puppies listed or waiting lists for future litters. Their contact information should also be listed, so don't hesitate to contact them.

Reputable breeders are passionate about their dogs and will want to know as much about you as you do about them. They want to make sure that their dogs are going to the right homes and will be happy to answer any questions you may have. If a breeder seems hesitant to discuss particular topics or produce certain records, this may be a red flag that they have something to hide. Be particularly wary about breeders who discourage you from visiting their homes and meeting their dogs. Some breeders may be cautious about bringing strangers into their homes when they have young, unvaccinated puppies in the house, but they'll likely explain the situation rather than act strangely. Most breeders are open and willing to discuss their dogs with potential owners. Use your best judgment when deciding whether you trust the person you're talking to. If you feel that they are a trustworthy and reputable breeder, set up a time to meet them in person and discuss their dogs and what you're looking for in your new puppy.

Health Tests and Certifications

As a general rule, reputable breeders regularly test their breeding dogs for common genetic disorders. They test their dogs to improve the breed as a whole and reduce the frequency of genetic diseases that are common to the breed. If a dog does not pass all of the required testing, it is generally spayed or neutered to prevent the condition from being passed on to future generations. Genetic testing is often necessary because certain conditions may allow a dog to carry the genes for a disease without showing any symptoms itself. A reputable breeder who is passionate about the breed works hard to improve the health and quality of life of their dogs with every generation. Regular health testing not only allows them to keep track of the health of their dogs, but it provides solid proof that the dogs are as healthy as the breeders say they are.

The Orthopedic Foundation for Animals (OFA) is one of the top institutions in canine genetic research. Their publicly accessible online database contains the test results of thousands of dogs of almost every breed. The database is continually expanding based on the results submitted to the OFA by breeders and owners. For a nominal fee, the OFA will examine and rate test results before adding them to their database, known as the Canine Health Information Center (CHIC). Most tests require dogs to be fully grown, and some tests must be repeated throughout the dog's lifetime to maintain certification. The OFA's website has a list of hundreds of breeds and recommended tests for each breed, along with frequency of testing and recommended age at the time of testing. Dogs who submit all of the required tests receive an identification number, or CHIC number, that can be searched for on the OFA website.

The OFA requires Rhodesian Ridgebacks to be tested for a number of conditions in order to receive their CHIC number. Ridgebacks must be tested after the age of twelve months for hip and elbow dysplasia. They must also receive an annual eye exam every year up to age nine by an ophthalmologist approved by the American College of Veterinary Ophthalmologists (ACVO). Ridgebacks must be tested annually for autoimmune thyroiditis from ages two to six, and again at age eight. Optional tests include a cardiac exam after one year of age and a hearing exam.

*Photo Courtesy of
Anne Rosén*

Breeder Contracts and Guarantees

An important and necessary aspect of purchasing a purebred dog is the breeder contract or guarantee. This legally binding contract protects both you and the breeder, while prioritizing the health and well-being of the puppy you're purchasing. The contract contains agreements between you and the breeder such as the price paid and vaccinations given to the puppy, as well as what happens if the puppy falls ill or does not meet the standards outlined in the contract. Some breeders also choose to require adopters to feed the dog a certain type of food. Avid supporters of raw diets will often only allow their puppies to go to homes that will continue feeding them raw diets. Breeders of performance or sport dogs may also require potential adopters to show or compete with their dogs and their requirements may be stated within the contract.

Contracts should contain a clause guaranteeing a puppy's health. If all required testing has been done on the parents, the contract may state that the puppy should be free of any serious genetic diseases or disorders. If a puppy tests positive for a genetic disease later in life, a clause within the contract should also state what steps should be taken by the breeder and owner. Some owners may fall in love with their puppy regardless of health, but some may opt to return the dog to the breeder in exchange for the purchase price or a new puppy from a different litter.

Most breeder contracts or guarantees will also state that the breeder is willing to take the dog back at any time and for any reason. Should you not be able to care for the dog at any time during its life, the breeder will likely want to ensure that the dog doesn't end up in a shelter or an unapproved home. Dogs in shelters often face higher risks of injury, illness, and even euthanasia. Most reputable breeders are willing to take a dog back with no questions asked. There may also be a "happiness clause" within the contract, which states that if you are not happy with your puppy for any reason you may return it to the breeder. Whether or not you will receive a refund under these circumstances should also be documented.

By signing the breeder's contract, you are agreeing to accept the responsibility of the puppy's lifelong health and happiness. If the contract requires you to spay or neuter the dog at a certain age, or compete in certain sports, by signing the contract you are legally agreeing to do so. Some breeders also include a clause stating that a certain portion of the purchase price will be returned to the owner upon proof that specific actions have been taken.

The breeder will usually provide the contract before you take possession of the puppy. Be sure to read the contract thoroughly and take note of any questions you have. If you would like to add, change, or discuss anything, be sure to do so before you sign the contract. Both you and the breeder need to be in complete agreement before signing this legally binding paperwork. Remember, the contract is not meant to complicate the purchasing process, it's simply intended to keep the puppy's best interests in mind while protecting both the buyer and breeder.

Choosing the Perfect Puppy

Choosing your ideal puppy out of a litter of adorable Rhodesian Ridgebacks can seem like a daunting task, but discussing your needs with the breeder can help you make the right decision. No one knows that particular litter of puppies better than the breeder, so he or she will be an invaluable source of information when it comes to choosing the right puppy.

It's essential that you look past the appearance of a puppy

> **QUOTE**
> **"Puppy Finder"**
>
> The Rhodesian Ridgeback Club of the United States (rrcus.org) is the parent club "dedicated to the preservation, protection, and advancement of the breed." On this website you'll find guidelines for the breed standard, pertinent information regarding health testing, and reputable breeders.

when choosing your Rhodesian Ridgeback. Although there is not a huge variety in color or markings in the breed, it's still important to place the puppy's appearance at the bottom of your wish list. Instead, the puppy's temperament should be a priority, especially if you are looking for a family or competition dog. Meeting the parents of the litter should give you an idea of what the puppies will be like when they grow up. If you intend to compete with your dog, you'll also need to consider conformation and athletic ability. Regardless of what you intend to do with your Ridgeback, it's important that you remain open-minded about the dog's appearance and take all of a dog's characteristics into consideration.

Pay attention to the personalities of the puppies. Even at a relatively young age, their natural dispositions will be apparent. If you want an outgoing, sociable puppy, you may want to choose one that approaches you boldly and confidently rather than one that sits away from the group in a shy or fearful manner. High-energy puppies will likely be bouncing around with their littermates and visitors while lower-energy dogs may be more interested in relaxing by your side. Seeking the breeder's opinion will help you to decide which personality suits you best, since he or she will have the best knowledge of each puppy's temperament.

Tips for Adopting a Rhodesian Ridgeback

Adopting a Rhodesian Ridgeback from a shelter or rescue organization is always a great option, especially if you're looking for a family companion rather than a competitive show dog. If you've decided to adopt rather than buy, it's still important that you have some idea of what you're looking for in a dog. Most shelters and rescues test their dogs' temperaments and assess their level of training, so they have a better idea of what type of lifestyle they need. Many rescues also have dogs in foster homes, rather than kennels, so their foster family will have a good understanding of what the dog is like outside of a shelter environment. Knowing what kind of lifestyle you lead and what your goals are for your new dog will help you and the rescue staff make the right decision.

Before committing to adoption, you need to decide whether you're willing to take on any behavioral or health challenges. Many dogs end up in rescue because their previous families were unable or unwilling to deal with certain issues. Additionally, if dogs are passed from home to home, they can often develop bad habits or their training may have simply been ne-

Photo Courtesy of
Charlene Walsh

glected. Consider specific bad habits and decide whether or not each be-havior is a deal-breaker. A lack of socialization or housetraining can be eas-ily solved, but aggressive behavior can be more of a challenge to correct.

If you have kids or other pets at home, remember to mention them to staff. Some Rhodesian Ridgebacks can be fearful or aggressive with children or other animals, especially if they've had bad experiences in their previous homes. To prevent disaster or a return to the shelter it's crucial to make sure early on that your new family member is comfortable around your kids or other pets. Most organizations will require a formal introduction be-tween the dog and your children or pets to make sure everyone gets along. A carefully supervised introduction is essential to the beginning of a healthy new relationship.

Most shelters and rescues will require a formal application before adopting a pet. The application form will likely ask for a variety of informa-tion about your lifestyle and home. For instance, they may ask if you live in an apartment without access to a yard or in the country with unfenced property, how many members of your family are in your household, and how long the dog will be left alone every day. Some organizations also do a home check, which is usually performed by one of their volunteers. A home check involves a rescue volunteer coming to your home to make sure it's a safe environment for a dog. They may suggest certain changes, such as fix-ing a hole in the fence, before you are approved for adoption. Volunteers are usually quite forgiving and will happily give you a chance to make your home safe before bringing home your new family member.

CHAPTER 3

Preparing Your Home for Your New Rhodesian Ridgeback

Adjusting Your Current Pets and Children

It may seem daunting to introduce your new Rhodesian Ridgeback to your existing household, but with safety as a priority, it can be done easily and with little preparation. It's crucial that you remember that existing family members, both human and animal, may need some time to adjust to the new addition, so patience is key. You may need to closely supervise interactions for several days or weeks before everyone can be trusted to be left alone together, so go slowly and don't rush the introductions.

A small area with little traffic, such as a laundry room, is ideal for your new dog's personal space. Setting up a separate space for your Rhodesian Ridgeback will allow her to adjust to your household with minimal stress.

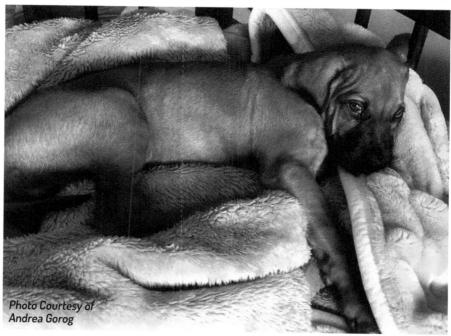

Photo Courtesy of
Andrea Gorog

Rather than shutting the door, which may make your Ridgeback feel isolated, you can install a removable gate, such as those intended for toddlers. Such gates are usually pressure-mounted, which means they don't need to be screwed or nailed into your walls or doorframes. Playpens or exercise pens work well too, especially if you're using only a portion of a larger space. The purpose of the barrier is to allow new and existing family members to have their own space to retreat to if they become overwhelmed. The barrier prevents close interactions, which may lead to accidents or injuries, but still allows everyone to see and smell each other. Over time, this allows the new dog to become part of the family with as little stress as possible.

Once your Rhodesian Ridgeback has begun to settle into his new home, you can start introducing her to your existing family members. Ideally, introductions should take place on neutral territory and with only one person or animal at a time. This can help reduce the chances of anyone becoming overwhelmed and reacting badly. If the weather permits, introducing your new dog to your existing household can be done outdoors. If your puppy hasn't been fully vaccinated yet, or you have indoor-only pets such as cats, a less frequently used room of the house works best, such as a guest room or formal dining room. This helps prevent your existing pets from becoming territorial over their favorite room or area. Generally, Rhodesian Ridgebacks get along well with others, but if you sense tension between your new dog and your existing pets, take a step back and try again at a later time. They may simply need more time to familiarize themselves with each other from a safe distance. Some pets can be a little resistant to change, especially when that change comes in the form of a bouncy, playful Rhodesian Ridgeback puppy. Go slowly and don't rush introductions, as this is the beginning of a lifelong relationship.

Once you've introduced your new Ridgeback to your family, you can begin allowing them to interact more frequently. Even if your Rhodesian Ridgeback is fully housetrained, it's best to allow her only into one room at a time, with supervision, at least until you know she can be trusted not to relieve herself or chew on furniture or other items. You may need to supervise your Ridgeback during her interactions with your family and pets for several weeks until you are certain that they can be trusted together. Accidents can and do happen, and close supervision during the early stages of introductions can help prevent such tragedies.

Dangerous Things That Dogs Might Eat

HELPFUL TIP
Counter Surfers

Do not leave food unattended and within reach of your Ridgeback. They can and will eat anything in sight. They also have a strong prey drive, so keep your dog in a safely enclosed area for their protection and the protection of smaller animals. Prepare to spend consistent time training your Ridgeback to allow it to grow into a faithful and protective friend.

Before bringing your Rhodesian Ridgeback home for the first time, you should go through each room of your house to make sure it's safe for your new family member. Puppies tend to explore their world using their mouths and the average household is full of potential dangers.

Some of the biggest dangers to young puppies are poisons intended for insects, rodents, and other pests. Such poisons are usually made to appeal to the animals they target, but they may also attract the eye of curious puppies. If you are struggling with a pest problem, it may be helpful to ask a pest control professional for advice on how to deal with your infestation without potentially endangering your pets. There are many different methods of pest control that are safer to use around pets than poison.

Before allowing your Rhodesian Ridgeback into your garage or any area where a car may be parked, be sure that the area is free of antifreeze. Antifreeze has a sweet taste, so dogs and other animals may try to lick up the substance if they find it. Ethylene glycol is the toxic ingredient in antifreeze and even small amounts can be deadly, so be sure to clean up any antifreeze leaks immediately and repair any leaks to prevent your dog or any other neighborhood pet from being poisoned. Symptoms of antifreeze poisoning include wobbly or drunken movement, vomiting, diarrhea, rapid heartbeat, seizures, and fainting. If you suspect your pet has consumed antifreeze, contact your local vet immediately.

If you have children, it's important that you keep their toys away from your curious new puppy. Rhodesian Ridgebacks will readily play with children's toys if they find them. Unfortunately, toys intended for children are often not built to withstand a dog's teeth and your puppy may destroy the toy and possibly ingest small pieces. These small pieces of toy can create an intestinal blockage, which can be deadly without surgical intervention. Even toys intended for dogs can be chewed or broken, so keep a close eye on your dog's toys, too, and remove them once they've been chewed down to a small size or had pieces broken off.

Although beautiful, houseplants can be dangerous to curious puppies. Some puppies may show no interest in plants, while others will readily gobble up a plant if allowed to. If you have a collection of houseplants, try to keep only nontoxic plants, such as Christmas cacti and snake plants, or keep them out of your puppy's reach. Even adult Rhodesian Ridgebacks have been known to nibble on houseplants, so be careful about what kind of plants you bring into your home.

An unexpected source of danger can be found in your kitchen. Trash cans can contain any number of dangerous items and must be kept away from your Rhodesian Ridgeback. Common dangers include cooked bones, toxic foods, broken items, and plastic. Unfortunately, the leftover food in trash cans can be quite enticing to a dog, so you may need to get creative to keep your dog out of the trash. Keeping your trash can inside a cabinet can be helpful, but some dogs may still figure out how to open the cabinet door. In this case, cabinet door locks intended for toddlers can be helpful. Some trash cans can also be locked. That said, it's best to keep your dog from discovering the delights of the trash can in the first place, as scrounging in the garbage for scraps can be a difficult habit to break once it has started.

Photo Courtesy of Steve Warwick

Other Household Dangers

Photo Courtesy of Sandy Gilbert

Power cords can also present a danger to Rhodesian Ridgeback puppies. Puppies may try to chew a cord to relieve some of the discomfort of teething, and they can be seriously injured or even killed. Until your puppy is old enough and responsible enough to be trusted alone in the house, be sure to supervise her at all times. If you cannot provide supervision, leave her in her designated area or crate to keep her safe. Remove all power cords from within your puppy's reach before allowing her into a new room. It may be helpful to get down onto her level to see what she is able to reach so you have a better idea of what needs to be removed from her space.

Household chemicals are another area of concern when preparing your home for your new arrival. Make sure there are no cleaning supplies, medication, or gardening chemicals within your Ridgeback's reach. If your puppy has a habit of getting into cabinets, you may want to invest in cabinet locks that are designed to keep toddlers out. If you suspect your puppy has ingested a dangerous substance, contact your vet or local poison control hotline immediately. The sooner your puppy receives treatment, the more likely it is that he'll survive the ordeal.

Preparing a Space for Your Rhodesian Ridgeback Inside

Choosing a space for your puppy is the first step in preparing your home for your new family member. The space will provide a safe area for your puppy to live for the next few weeks or months, until he can be trusted to have access to your entire home. Rooms with easy-to-clean floors such as laundry rooms, guest bathrooms, or even kitchens work well. Smaller spaces are ideal for puppies to limit the space they have. Dogs don't usually like to relieve themselves close to their food or sleeping areas, so smaller spaces can help with housetraining. You can also choose to set up a crate within the small room or area. If possible, try to choose a room that is near the center of your family's activities. This way, your puppy will be able to see the action and not feel so isolated, but will be able to retreat to his own space if he feels overwhelmed.

After you've decided which room your puppy will stay in, it's time to puppy-proof the space. Remove any dangers such as power cords, house-plants, or anything harmful that your Ridgeback may be able to get into. It can be helpful to get down on the floor at the puppy's level to see what he might be able to reach. While puppy-proofing, it's also important to make sure the area is secure. Make sure your dog can't escape from his playpen or squeeze through any pressure-mounted gates. Any doors to the outside should be locked to prevent them from being left open on accident.

Once the area is safe and secure, set up your puppy's supplies. If you're using disposable puppy pads, lay them out over the floor. Not only will they help with cleanup if your puppy has an accident, but they'll also help with any messes made from spilled food or water dishes. It's much easier to dis-pose of an absorbent puppy pad than it is to scrub a dirty floor. If you notice that your Ridgeback is chewing on or shredding her puppy pads, you may need to remove them to prevent accidental ingestion.

When deciding where to place your dog's bedding, choose a location that is somewhat out of the way. This will give your dog a safe place to re-treat to if the daily activities of your household overwhelm her during her first few days in her new home. As she adjusts, you can always move the bed closer to the entrance of his space so that she can relax while still keep-ing an eye on the family. As with the puppy pads, make sure your puppy isn't chewing on any of her bedding. Fabric and stuffing can easily become a choking hazard or a potential intestinal blockage if swallowed.

The ideal place for your dog's food and water dishes is the quietest cor-ner of her area. Placing the dishes away from her bedding will help prevent her bedding from being soiled if she accidentally knocks her bowls over. Avoid using any area near the entrance of his space, if possible. Your new Ridgeback may become excited when you come home after work or when you take her out for a walk and she may spill her food or water during her excitement. You may need to use trial and error for a few days to figure out the perfect layout of your dog's space.

Photo Courtesy of
Jonathan Higdon

Preparing Outside Spaces

The first step in preparing your yard or garden for the arrival of your Rhodesian Ridgeback is to walk along your fence to make sure there aren't any holes or weak spots through which he could escape. Just as you did with your indoor space, you may want to get down on the dog's level to see any areas where he may try to squeeze through. A loose dog is at risk of being hit by cars, killed by wild animals, or stolen, so make sure your fence is secure before allowing your new dog to play outside.

If you have a pool on your property, make sure that your new dog can't access the pool area without supervision. Some pool fencing may allow puppies to squeeze through the gaps, so make sure that your dog can't accidentally end up in the water. Although Rhodesian Ridgebacks are quite good swimmers, suddenly falling in water can cause a dog to panic and not be able to find his way out. If you think your dog could squeeze through the fence, you may want to line the lower half of your pool's fence with chicken wire or garden fencing to keep him out.

Depending on the landscaping of your yard, or the type of garden you keep, you may want to double-check that all plants in your yard are non-toxic to dogs.

Supplies

Before bringing your Rhodesian Ridgeback home from the shelter or breeder, it can be helpful to compile a list of the supplies you'll need during your first few days or weeks together. Introducing a new dog to your existing household will be nerve-wracking enough without the added stress of forgetting to buy dog food. If you have other dogs in your home, you will likely only need to buy a few new items, but it can still be helpful to write everything down.

The most important item to have ready for your new dog is dog food. Find out what your Ridgeback is currently eating at the shelter or at the breeder's home. If that food isn't what you'd like to feed, you'll still need enough of the old food to make a smooth transition to your food of choice. Changing foods too quickly can cause digestive upset, which can cause unnecessary stress during your first few days together. If you're bringing home an adult dog, be sure to ask about any food allergies or sensitivities. Training should start as soon as you bring your dog home, so be sure to pick up some training treats as well.

The second most important item to have ready for your new dog is an appropriately sized collar with identification. Depending on the size and age of your new Ridgeback, you may need to estimate what size to buy. Most collars are adjustable so you should be able to guess what size will work best. Most pet stores or online retailers also sell identification tags or plates that you can customize with your contact information. Proper identification is essential in case your puppy should escape from his new home and become lost. In the beginning, most experts recommend a simple nylon or leather leash. Extendable leashes work for some, but they are often too long and unruly, especially during the early days of training. Regular leashes less than six feet in length are ideal for keeping excitable puppies under control and out of danger.

A comfortable bed should also be on your shopping list. Your dog should have somewhere cozy to retreat to during the transition into her new home, so be sure to pick a bed that is appropriately sized and padded. Adult and senior dogs often enjoy thicker, firmer beds, while puppies enjoy snuggling into fluffy beds and blankets. If you're bringing home a puppy, it might be best not to splurge on an expensive bed just yet. Puppies often chew up their first bed or two during their teething stages and it can be frustrating if you've spent a lot of money on a nice memory foam bed only to see it torn into shreds.

No matter what type of bed you buy, try to get something with a removable cover. Although the entire bed will need to be washed on occasion, it's nice to be able to just wash the cover when needed. If your dog enjoys burrowing under or snuggling into blankets, fleece blankets are an inexpensive option.

The same rule applies to your puppy's first toys. Try to find inexpensive toys that are good for chewing. Giving your dog appropriate toys can help reduce the chances of her chewing on a valuable item in your home. Remember, toys should be large enough that your dog can't swallow them whole. Regardless of size, you'll need to keep an eye on your Ridgeback's toys to make sure she hasn't broken or chewed off small pieces that she could swallow.

Rhodesian Ridgebacks are low-maintenance dogs in terms of grooming needs, but a few grooming supplies will help keep your dog looking and smelling great. A rubber curry comb is a great option to help remove dead hair, both on a dry coat or in the bath. You may also want to invest in a quality shampoo in case your puppy gets dirty or begins to smell. If you intend to clip your dog's nails at home, you'll also need a nail clipper or grinder. If you're unsure of what grooming supplies will work best with your dog, ask your local groomer for recommendations.

Lastly, if you're bringing home a Rhodesian Ridgeback that hasn't been housetrained yet, you'll want to bring home a few items to help with training. Absorbent, disposable puppy pads are helpful with cleanup, especially when used to line playpens or your dog's designated room. Depending on the type of flooring in your home, you'll also want to purchase some type of cleaning solution. Most pet stores and online retailers offer a variety of products intended to clean various types of flooring. Many cleaners contain enzymes to help eliminate odor and discourage your dog from relieving himself in that same area again. Many owners also choose to hang bells on their door during housetraining. The idea is that the dog will learn to nudge or paw the bells when he needs to go outside, letting you know he's ready to go out before he has an accident.

CHAPTER 4

Bringing Home Your New Rhodesian Ridgeback

The Importance of Having a Plan

It's important to thoroughly plan the arrival of your Rhodesian Ridgeback to help reduce the stress of the transition for both your new dog and your family. If you bring your puppy home only to realize that you haven't purchased any supplies or set up her designated area, you're only creating a stressful environment that may scare or overwhelm an already nervous puppy. Proper planning will help make the first few days go more smoothly and allow you to bond with your new dog rather than worry about what to do with her.

If you already have other dogs at home, you may not need to plan quite as thoroughly, as you likely already have most of the necessary supplies and have also had the experience of bringing home other dogs and may already know what to expect. If you're a new dog owner, running into problems in the first few days with your new dog can cause you to panic if you haven't thoroughly planned things out. Figuring out a plan and writing it down will give you a helpful resource to refer to when things go awry. For example, planning out your dog's first car ride home will allow you to focus on safe driving rather than on the carsick puppy running loose in the back seat. Adding a new member to the family can be an overwhelming experience, but being prepared will help you to focus on building a lifelong relationship instead of worrying about what could go wrong.

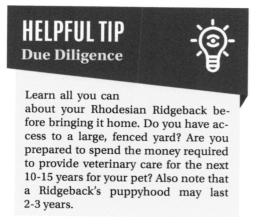

HELPFUL TIP
Due Diligence

Learn all you can about your Rhodesian Ridgeback before bringing it home. Do you have access to a large, fenced yard? Are you prepared to spend the money required to provide veterinary care for the next 10-15 years for your pet? Also note that a Ridgeback's puppyhood may last 2-3 years.

The Ride Home

The most important aspect of your Rhodesian Ridgeback's first time in the car is your energy and your reaction to the event. Your dog will probably travel in a car many time during his life, so it's important to make a positive impression on him during his first trip. Bringing home a new family member can be exciting, but you need to stay calm and collected to encourage your puppy to do the same. If you act nervous or excited, your puppy may think he also needs to be nervous about riding in the car.

Another essential part of riding in the car is proper restraint. You must wear a seatbelt in the car to protect yourself in case of an accident and your dog should be no different. An unrestrained dog can easily panic and distract you from driving or leap onto your lap. If you have an accident, he may be able to escape the car and run out into traffic. It's much safer to have your dog properly restrained in the car until you reach your destination. Depending on your dog's preferences as well as your own, there are many types of safe restraints on the market. For puppies, the best option is a crate or carrier. Many soft-sided carriers also have straps that allow a seatbelt to be passed through to secure the carrier to the seat. Other types of crates fit snugly into either the back seat or cargo area to prevent the crate from moving around the car. Metal or mesh barriers are also available to keep your dog contained in the back seat or cargo area. Older, more experienced dogs may also enjoy wearing a harness with a seatbelt attachment. Use your best judgment to decide what method to use on your Ridgeback's first ride home. You can always change your mind later if you'd like to try another method.

No matter which type of restraint you choose to use, it's important to be prepared for any possible carsickness. Many dogs who are inexperienced travelers can become carsick, especially if the road has a lot of curves or changes in altitude. Lining your dog's crate or carrier with towels can be helpful, as can absorbent puppy pads. If you choose to use barriers or seatbelts, you can also invest in waterproof seat covers. You may want to bring a few extra towels or blankets to aid in cleanup, as well as a bag to store any soiled linens.

Riding in the car can be a frightening experience for some dogs and they may react badly. Until you know how your dog reacts in the car, proper restraint is even more necessary. Some dogs may bark or cry, soil themselves, or try to escape. Containing a dog in a crate will help to restrain her, but it may also give her a sense of security. Some dogs also calm down if a blanket or towel is placed over the crate, giving them a secluded sense of comfort. Remaining calm during these times is essential. If you react to your dog's panic, you're only confirming her worries that something is wrong. Bringing a small blanket or toy with you from your dog's breeder or foster family can help comfort her during the ride. The familiar smell may soothe her during this stressful transition.

The First Night Home

The first night home with your Rhodesian Ridgeback may be somewhat sleepless for you, so it's best you bring your new dog home on a weekend or day off. This is especially true if you're bringing home a puppy. This will be the first time a puppy spends the night away from his littermates, so he may become upset. Even if you're bringing home an adult dog, the change can be enough to cause distress.

Before you bring your new dog home, you need to decide where he will spend his first night. Although there will likely be a lot of howling and barking, it's generally not recommended to keep your dog somewhere out

Photo Courtesy of
Steve Warwick

of earshot. As tempting as it may be to actually get some rest, the isolation will only cause him to cry more and you won't hear him if he gets into trouble or needs to go outside. Keeping your dog in a crate somewhere near your own bed is probably the best option. If he's in a crate, he will be unable to relieve himself in your bed or bedroom or chew up your furniture or personal items in frustration. However, he'll still be able to let you know if he needs to go outside and will be comforted by your presence.

Photo Courtesy of Mike Krzyza

It's crucial that you take your puppy outside to go to the bathroom just before bedtime. The later you can take him out, the more sleep you'll be able to get before he needs to go out again. You'll also need to make sure that taking him outside is the first thing you do after getting up. If you're bringing home a puppy, you'll need to take him out every few hours during the night. You'll need to develop the ability to distinguish his cries for attention from his cries to go outside. This may be difficult during the first night, so try to keep to a strict schedule of taking him out every few hours.

If your Rhodesian Ridgeback cries after you've brought him inside or is obviously crying for attention, it's important that you ignore him as much as possible. When you first put him in his crate before bed, he may bark or become upset, but you must ignore him so that he begins to develop a nightly routine. It may be difficult to ignore a barking dog when you're trying to get to sleep, but acknowledging him will only encourage him to act out when he's unhappy. Eventually, he'll give up and fall asleep.

First Vet Visit/Choosing a Vet

Photo Courtesy of Beth Keener

Your Rhodesian Ridgeback's first visit to the vet will set the tone for a lifetime of vet visits, so be sure to make it a positive experience for all. Even if your new dog isn't quite ready for his next round of vaccines, you should take her to visit the vet within her first few days in your home, just to make sure she's healthy and is handling the transition well. Many breeders require this in their contracts, as it helps to ensure that they are keeping their end of the deal by sending you home with a healthy puppy.

If you don't already have a veterinarian, the best way to find a reputable one is to ask friends and family who own dogs. Many owners can be quite opinionated about the clinic that they will and will not use, but they will readily recommend someone they know and trust. If you have gotten your puppy from a local breeder or shelter, they may also be able to recommend a vet based on their own experiences. Once you've chosen a vet, be sure to ask about their emergency hours. If clinic staff are not available around the clock, they may be able to recommend a reputable emergency veterinary clinic to consult if something happens outside their normal hours.

During your puppy's first visit to the vet, she will undergo a physical exam. During this exam, the vet or veterinary technician will weigh the dog, listen to her heart and lungs, and check her temperature. Your puppy's eyes, ears, teeth, and abdomen will also be examined to make sure she's in good health. The veterinary staff may also ask if your puppy is eating, drinking, and relieving herself normally.

It's likely your vet will talk to you about which vaccines your puppy will receive during this visit and when you need to bring him back for more. The vet may also discuss any potential allergic reactions your dog may have to the vaccines. Most dogs handle vaccines well, but it's important to keep an eye out for any type of reaction so that proper treatment can be administered as soon as possible. If you notice any hives, swelling of the injection site or muzzle, or difficulty breathing, your dog needs to be treated immediately. Many vets ask that you wait around the clinic for 15-20 minutes to make sure your dog doesn't have any adverse reaction.

It's common for veterinary staff to also perform fecal exams on puppies as well as dogs coming from shelters. Even if your Ridgeback isn't showing any symptoms of a parasitic infection, it's still important to make sure she's healthy. Roundworms are a common occurrence, especially in young puppies. Thankfully, if your dog tests positive for intestinal parasites, treatment is generally easy and inexpensive.

Your puppy's first vet visit is an excellent time to discuss microchipping. Microchipping is a simple procedure in which a small microchip, about the size of a grain of rice, is inserted beneath your dog's skin over his withers. The microchip can be scanned by any approved scanner and will help to reunite you with your dog should he become lost. Unlike collars and ID tags, microchips cannot fall off, so it's a great way to ensure that your dog can be identified. Just be sure to update your contact information with the microchip company to make sure they have your most recent phone number and address should these ever change.

You should also discuss the proper time to spay or neuter your puppy with your veterinarian. Most vets recommend performing the surgery at around six months of age, but your vet will be able to make a more accurate recommendation based on your dog's size, weight, and overall health. You'll be able to get an estimate of the cost of the procedure so that you can budget accordingly if necessary. If you have any concerns about the procedure or about your dog undergoing anesthesia, now is the time to mention them. Modern anesthesia techniques are incredibly safe, but your vet will be able to answer any questions you may have.

Puppy Classes

Teaching your Rhodesian Ridgeback to be a responsible member of your family and the community is an important part of puppyhood. To help your Ridgeback reach his potential, you might want to attend puppy classes. It may not be a problem to have your puppy pulling on the leash or jumping up on your leg now, but as an adult those behaviors can be dangerous. The sooner you begin teaching your dog good manners, the better. Puppy classes are simply basic obedience classes, but they tend to focus more on the short attention span and curious nature of puppies. Your puppy will learn basic commands, such as sit and stay, and you'll be able to get the profes-

Photo Courtesy of
Caroline Higgins

sional advice of a trainer on any problems you may be struggling with, such as housetraining or bad habits. Puppy classes are also a great place to begin socializing your puppy with other dogs and people.

Most puppy classes will require your Ridgeback to be a certain age before she is allowed to attend. The reason for this is that most puppies will have been vaccinated several times by that age. You may still need to provide proof of vaccination before your first class. This is to keep all puppies in attendance healthy and free of communicable diseases.

You should be able to find plenty of different options for classes, depending on the area you live in. Most areas have private trainers or obedience schools that hold regular classes. Many pet stores and shelters also hold regular puppy and basic obedience classes. If you're unsure of where to look, try contacting your breeder, local shelter, or veterinarian, as they may be able to recommend a particular trainer or facility.

Most puppy classes are held as a group, as this can help with socialization. Many puppy classes have age limits, which is to help protect puppies from larger adult dogs should they show aggression. If you're bringing home an older dog, try looking for basic obedience classes rather than puppy classes. They will cover the same subjects, but will be directed more toward adult dogs instead of puppies. If your new dog has any bad habits or has not been socialized properly, you may want to search for one-on-one lessons with a local trainer. Group classes can be overwhelming to some dogs, so starting out with private lessons can be a great way to develop basic skills before you try attending group classes.

Cost Breakdown for the First Year

Dog ownership can be expensive, so if you're living on a particularly tight budget, you may want to reconsider bringing a dog into your life. However, many owners are able to take excellent care of their dogs on a tight budget because they've budgeted accordingly.

If you're buying a Rhodesian Ridgeback from a breeder, the initial purchase price will be one of your biggest costs in the first year of dog ownership. Depending on the quality, area, and potential of the puppy, you'll likely spend somewhere between several hundred to several thousand dollars. If you're adopting a dog from a shelter, your initial adoption fee will probably be a few hundred dollars at most. However, adoption fees also usually cover vaccinations, deworming, and spaying or neutering. If you're buying a dog from a breeder you'll need to cover those costs yourself.

Mandatory expenses such as food, veterinary care, and supplies, can add up quickly. Depending on where you live, you could be spending between $900 and $3,500 just for basic care. The following table contains an estimate of the cost of the first year of Rhodesian Ridgeback ownership:

Mandatory Expenses	Cost Estimate
Food	$300 - $900
Food and Water Dishes	$10 - $50
Treats	$50 - $150
Toys	$20 - $200
Collars and Leashes	$10 - $100
Crate	$25 - $100
Dog Beds	$25 - $100
Vaccines and Routine Veterinary Care	$100 - $350
Heartworm Testing	$10 - $35
Heartworm Prevention	$25 - $125
Flea and Tick Prevention	$40 - $200
Spaying or Neutering	$150 - $600
Puppy Classes	$200 - $500
Total	$965 - $3410

Unfortunately, those are not the only costs that you may encounter in the first year with your Rhodesian Ridgeback. Although Ridgebacks are short-haired, they still need regular grooming and many owners find it difficult or impossible to bathe a large dog at home. Professional grooming costs will vary according your area and the services you choose, but they can add up to several hundred dollars per year.

If you plan on traveling without your new dog, you'll also need to consider the cost of having someone care for him in your absence. You may choose to drop your dog off at a boarding facility or have a pet sitter care for your dog either in their home or in yours. The price for these services will range from around $15 per day to over $100 per day. If you have friends or family who are dog lovers, you may be able to ask them to care for your beloved Ridgeback in your absence and offer to watch their dog the next time they leave town.

The biggest potential expense you face as a dog owner is emergency veterinary care. Although you can do your absolute best to keep your Rhodesian Ridgeback safe and healthy, accidents and illness can and will happen. Emergency care can range in cost from a few hundred dollars to several thousand or more. Pet insurance is one option that owners have to help cover the cost of emergency care. Many owners also choose to set aside a small amount every month to have available should an emergency occur.

Possible Expenses	Cost Estimate
Professional Grooming	$100 - $500
Emergency Veterinary Services	$200 - $1000+
Pet Sitting or Boarding	$15 - $100+ per day

The numbers listed in this section may make you feel somewhat overwhelmed, but it's important to understand that caring for an animal is a big financial responsibility. By bringing this dog into your home, you're accepting the responsibility of caring for her to the best of your abilities. Before bringing your Rhodesian Ridgeback home, you need to carefully consider whether you are ready for such a commitment. Regardless of your financial situation, careful planning and budgeting can help you be prepared for the potential costs of dog ownership without undue strain on your finances.

CHAPTER 5

Being a Puppy Parent

Standing by Your Expectations

Deciding to bring a Rhodesian Ridgeback into your home is a big commitment and it's essential that you have realistic expectations. Raising a puppy is a full-time job. The more time you're willing to commit to your new dog's training and development, the more quickly you're going to see progress. Housetraining and basic manners require consistency and if you aren't willing to dedicate the time and energy to teaching your dog the rules of the household, you may end up with an unruly and unmanageable dog.

During the first few weeks or months with your puppy, you should keep your expectations relatively low. Introducing a new dog into the family can be a stressful experience for everyone, so while you should definitely start training right away, you should also remember that you're still getting to know each other. If you set your expectations too high, you may become frustrated or disappointed with your Ridgeback's progress. Remember, the transition into a new household is a stressful time in your puppy's life and he'll need time to adjust before he can fully focus on training.

How to Crate Train

Crate training is essential to any dog's life, whether he's destined for the show ring or just a respectful member of the community. Even if you don't intend to keep your dog in a crate as an adult dog, waiting quietly in a crate is still a necessary skill. Your local groomer or veterinary clinic staff will likely need to put your dog in a cage at some point and it will be less stressful for everyone involved if he understands that he needs to wait quietly until he's asked to come out. There may also be an emergency situation in which you'll need to crate your dog for his own safety or the safety of others. A dog who hasn't been properly crate trained may try to bolt out the door, soil himself, or attempt to escape. He may injure himself by chewing or pawing at the sides of the kennel. In addition to being a danger to himself, he could also injure someone else if bolts out the door. Owning a dog means that you're taking responsibility for an animal's behavior, even in the presence of other people, so proper crate training will not only benefit you but everyone else that has to handle your dog.

The first step in introducing the crate to your Rhodesian Ridgeback is to make it appealing. An empty crate with a hard plastic floor is hardly a place that your dog will enjoy spending his time. Try putting his favorite bed, blankets, or favorite toy inside (if you trust him not to destroy it). The more comfortable your dog's crate is, the more likely it is that he'll want to go inside on his own.

To encourage your dog to enter the crate, try tossing a few treats just inside the door. At first, he may only step inside long enough to grab the treat before backing out, but that's fine. As you practice, you can try tossing the treats toward the back of the crate to encourage him to step inside with all four feet. As he becomes more comfortable, you can try shutting the door behind him for just a second or two. Remember to praise him accordingly. As his crate training progresses, you can try locking the door and leaving him in the crate for longer periods of time. If he begins to cry or bark, try to let him calm down before releasing him. If you let him out while he's barking, he'll learn that he can be let out any time he wants if he barks. Remember, you're the pack leader and you get to decide when he gets to come out of the crate.

Chewing

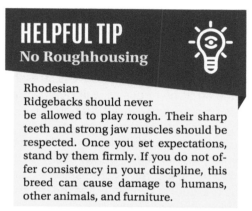

HELPFUL TIP
No Roughhousing

Rhodesian Ridgebacks should never be allowed to play rough. Their sharp teeth and strong jaw muscles should be respected. Once you set expectations, stand by them firmly. If you do not offer consistency in your discipline, this breed can cause damage to humans, other animals, and furniture.

Chewing is a destructive and dangerous habit for Rhodesian Ridgebacks to develop, but unfortunately, it's a normal part of puppyhood. However, it's important to discourage your dog from chewing on inappropriate items during this time to help prevent her from maintaining this bad habit as an adult. At around four months of age, your Ridgeback will begin to lose her puppy teeth. This process takes around two months and you can expect your puppy to have a mouth full of adult teeth by around six months of age. During the teething process, your puppy's gums will be quite sore and she may turn to chewing in an attempt to relieve some of her discomfort. She may try to chew furniture, shoes, children's toys, and even electrical cords, so you need to be diligent in keeping these things out of her reach.

To discourage your Ridgeback from chewing on your furniture or personal items, you may want to try one of the many products on the market designed to stop dogs from chewing. Typically, they can be sprayed directly on a variety of materials without stains or damage to the material. The sprays are usually sour, bitter, or spicy in flavor. The idea is that the dog will find the flavor so unpleasant that she will be deterred from chewing on an item. Just remember to reapply the spray occasionally so if your dog tries to chew the same item in the future, the unpleasant taste is still there to discourage her.

While you discourage your puppy from gnawing on inappropriate items, you also need to have plenty of appropriate options for her to chew on. Your local pet store or favorite online retailer will probably have a huge selection of chew toys to keep your dog busy and relieve her teething pain. There are even toys designed especially for teething puppies that can be frozen to help provide cooling relief for sore gums. All this chewing can wear down chew toys quickly, so be sure to keep an eye on your dog's toys to make sure she hasn't broken off any small pieces that may be accidentally swallowed.

Growling and Barking

The Rhodesian Ridgeback's natural confidence and wariness of strangers can lead to problems with aggression if left uncorrected. Puppies who feel insecure or unsure of a situation may growl or bark at strange people or dogs, but this must not be tolerated. It might be cute or funny for an eight-week-old puppy to growl at your neighbor, but when that puppy is a full-grown adult, no one will appreciate such behavior.

If your puppy growls or barks in inappropriate situations, clap loudly or use a sharp "No!" to distract him. Even if your puppy is reacting out of fear, it's important not to cuddle or attempt to soothe him. As tempting as it may be, reassuring your puppy will only let him know that he has a reason to be afraid and teach him that his reaction is appropriate. By distracting him or letting him know his behavior is unacceptable, you are teaching him that you have control of the situation and that he doesn't need to worry. Once he stops barking, you can reward him with treats or praise. With consistent correction, your puppy will eventually learn that he doesn't need to growl at strangers and the need for correction will become more infrequent.

Digging

Digging is a destructive and dangerous habit for your Rhodesian Ridgeback to develop. Although some breeds, such as terriers, are more prone to this behavior, any breed can learn this bad habit. Dogs that dig not only damage your yard or garden, but they may also damage their nails or even ingest rocks, dirt, or sticks. In addition, they may also be able to dig beneath your fence and escape. If you have expensive landscaping, the damage done by a digging dog can be quite costly as well.

If your Ridgeback has begun digging while spending time outside, you'll need to supervise her every time she goes out into your yard or garden. Consistent correction is the only way to fix bad habits and if you occasionally let her get away with the behavior, it will take much longer to solve the problem. As with inappropriate growling or barking, when you catch your dog in the act of digging, simply clap your hands or tell her "No!" The loud and startling sound will be enough to stop her from digging and she may wander off to find something else to do. In the beginning, you may need to correct her several times during each outing, but over time the frequency of your corrections will be reduced.

Photo Courtesy of
Gail Krenn

Separation Anxiety

Separation anxiety is a serious condition that can be incredibly difficult to fix, so prevention is key. Rhodesian Ridgebacks can be quite loyal to their families and may develop any number of the behaviors associated with separation anxiety when they are left alone at home. Symptoms of separation anxiety include panting, drooling, pacing, and excessive barking. If left uncorrected, some dogs may develop more destructive behaviors such as chewing or relieving themselves in the house. In extreme cases, dogs may even try to escape the confines of their crate, yard, or house. These behaviors are not only damaging to your property, but they can also be dangerous to your dog. He may hurt himself, ingest something toxic, or escape your property. Depending on the severity of your Ridgeback's separation anxiety, you may need to consult a professional trainer or behaviorist.

The biggest step you can take toward preventing separation anxiety is not to make a big deal out of leaving your house. It can be hard not to acknowledge your dog's adorable face as you walk out the door, but it's best if you skip the dramatic goodbye. The same rule applies to your arrival, regardless of how long you've been gone. When you come home, simply ignore your dog and take your time putting your things away. If you get excited when you leave or return, you may inadvertently be rewarding his anxiety. Instead, you should remain calm and only acknowledge your dog once he's settled down. If you leave the house calmly and return calmly, he'll understand that there's no reason for him to worry while you're gone. You'll also experience the benefit of coming home to a mellow dog, rather than one who races through the house and knocks you over in excitement.

Running Away

The most important skill your Rhodesian Ridgeback can learn is the recall. Running away is a dangerous habit for your dog to develop for many reasons. If your dog bolts out the front door or gets away from you at the park, it can end in tragedy. Therefore, teaching your dog to come when called is essential, regardless of whether she's destined for dog sports or as a family companion. If you start early and use plenty of positive reinforcement, you have a much better chance of catching your dog if she decides to chase after that squirrel. Start in your home with few distractions and build up to more distracting environments. Leashes can be found in every possible length to help with recall training. If you're struggling with your dog's recall, you may want to consult a professional.

If your Ridgeback has a habit of ignoring you in the house, don't be afraid to attach a leash to her collar and let her drag it around. As long as she doesn't chew on the leash, it shouldn't bother her in the house, as long you supervise her. If he decides to ignore you when you call her, you can simply grab the leash and correct her behavior. This is especially handy if she tries to bolt out open doors as you can grab or step on the leash before she gets away from you.

Photo Courtesy of
Stephanie Egger

Bedtime

Developing a bedtime routine can take weeks or even months of repetition before your dog understands what is expected of him. Try to stick to the same routine every night to help your Ridgeback develop good bedtime habits. The most important aspect of your pre-bedtime ritual is to remain calm. This means no roughhousing, play sessions, or vigorous walks. Try to accomplish those tasks earlier in the day. The more you can do with your Ridgeback earlier in the day, the more tired and calm he will be by the evening.

Remember to take your Rhodesian Ridgeback out for a bathroom break as late as possible before bed. Many owners make this the last task of the day before heading to bed. Taking your dog out as late as possible will help him sleep through the night better. If he's a puppy, it means you'll be able to get at least a few hours of sleep before he needs to go out again. Rhodesian Ridgebacks are intelligent dogs and will quickly learn your routine, so try to take your dog out at the same time every night if possible.

The location of your dog's bed can also make a difference in how well he behaves at bedtime. If you can place your Ridgeback's bed, crate, or playpen somewhere near your own bed, you may find that he settles down more quickly. For many dogs, sleeping quietly is easier when they are near their family. As Rhodesian Ridgebacks are naturally protective, they'll find comfort in knowing that they are with their pack.

Photo Courtesy of Adam Sexton

Leaving Your Rhodesian Ridgeback Home Alone

The first few times you leave your Rhodesian Ridgeback home alone can be stressful, but with a little preparation, it can be a positive experience for both you and your dog. Before leaving the house, make sure your Ridgeback is secure in his designated area or crate. Wherever you choose to leave your dog, be it a crate, playpen, or entire room, make sure there are no potential dangers. You've likely already puppy-proofed this area, but it doesn't hurt to take one more look around to be sure it's still safe.

To help your puppy adapt to being left alone, try leaving him alone for just short periods of time at first. It can be as simple as walking out your front door, waiting a few seconds, and then returning. As soon as he realizes that you aren't completely abandoning him, he should wait patiently for your return without worry. The first few times you leave, he may bark or whine, but this is normal. As he becomes more comfortable in your home, he'll start to relax in his space, even in your absence.

Leaving your house and returning in a calm manner are important steps in preventing separation anxiety. Don't worry about hurting your dog's feelings by leaving without saying goodbye. He'll be a more well-adjusted adult dog if he understands that your departure and arrival are nothing to worry about. Even if your dog does get excited when you come home from work or from running errands, it's important that you take your time and let him settle down before you say hello. Eventually, your Ridgeback won't worry about being left home alone and you will be able to leave the house knowing that he's happy and comfortable.

CHAPTER 6
Housetraining

Different Options for Housetraining

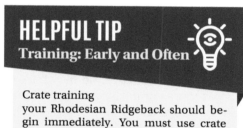

HELPFUL TIP
Training: Early and Often

Crate training your Rhodesian Ridgeback should begin immediately. You must use crate training when you are at home as well as when you are away. If this is accomplished, your dog will not associate the crate with you leaving it alone. For its comfort and health, always take your dog out before placing it in the crate.

Before you bring your new dog home, be it a puppy or an adult, you need to consider your options for housetraining. Even adult dogs who have been properly housetrained may have an accident or two while adjusting to their new living arrangements. Developing a housetraining plan will help you and your new dog adapt to a regular schedule, which will help your dog meet your training goals more quickly. The most common method of housetraining involves teaching the dog that the only appropriate place to relieve himself is outdoors. Some owners choose a certain spot in their yard, while others leave that choice to the dog.

Disposable puppy pads, litter boxes, or indoor potty patches are great options to supplement traditional housetraining, especially with young puppies and/or if you live in an extremely hot or cold climate. Unfortunately, indoor options can be a little more difficult with adult Rhodesian Ridgebacks. Ridgebacks are large dogs, and as such, they have rather large messes, which can be a hassle to clean up. That said, the younger your puppy, the more frequently he will need to go to the bathroom, and allowing him to have alternatives to going outside will help reduce the number of messes you'll need to clean up. Many Ridgeback owners choose to have one or more of these options available to their puppy, but still plan on taking him outside every few hours. Eventually, as the puppy learns what is expected of him, he will begin to use the indoor options less frequently and they can eventually be eliminated.

Another aspect of housetraining that you need to consider is how you plan on teaching your dog to signal that he needs to go outside. At first, close supervision will be necessary at all times so that if you see your dog circling, sniffing, or acting as if he needs to relieve himself you can rush him outside immediately. However, you may also want to give him the option of telling you when he needs to go out. Rhodesian Ridgebacks are incredibly intelligent dogs that can quickly learn how to tell you what they need. Many owners opt to hang bells on their doorknob that can be nudged by the dog and heard throughout the house. Some owners may prefer their dogs to paw at the door, but this can be damaging to certain types of doors. Others may simply reward their dog for sitting quietly by the door when he needs to go out. However you decide to teach your dog, you need to be consistent and reward him for displaying the correct behavior by taking him outside immediately.

Photo Courtesy of
Caroline Higgins

The First Few Weeks

The first few weeks with your new Rhodesian Ridgeback are crucial to her housetraining. If done properly, she can make great progress during this time, but if your training is inconsistent, you may see very little improvement. The more consistent you are in your daily routine, the more quickly you're going to see progress. At first, you will need to take your dog out every few hours to prevent her from relieving herself indoors. With time and consistent training, you'll be able to increase the time between trips outside. However, for the first few weeks, you should plan on taking her out every few hours and try to stick to the same daily schedule if possible.

The general rule of thumb for housetraining is that your dog can go one hour for every month of her age between potty breaks. For example, you can expect a four-month-old puppy to need to go outside approximately every four hours. You can always take your puppy out more frequently if you

desire but waiting any longer than this will almost guarantee a mess in the house. Unfortunately, this rule applies around the clock, so you can expect to have quite a few sleepless nights during the first few weeks with your puppy. However, once you develop a routine, you'll be better able to predict when your puppy will need to go outside and she should have fewer accidents in the house. Puppies respond well to routine, so it's important to try to stick to the same bathroom break schedule every day if possible.

It's crucial that you time your puppy's bathroom breaks right, especially during the first few weeks. Try to take your puppy outside as late as possible before bedtime and right away after waking up in the morning. You should also take her out immediately after returning home and after any meals. As you spend more time with your puppy, you'll learn her body language and will get better at anticipating her needs. Some puppies may need to go out immediately after meals, while others may need some time before they are ready for a potty break. Pay attention to your puppy's body language and adopt a schedule that works for you and your dog. As your adapt your schedule to your puppy's needs and she begins to understand what you expect from her, accidents in the house should become less frequent.

Positive Reinforcement

One of the most effective methods of training dogs is positive reinforcement. This method involves rewarding your dog with a positive stimulus, such as praise or food, when he performs a desired behavior. Positive reinforcement can be an effective aid in housetraining, especially during the early stages when your dog may be a little confused about your expectations. As with all other aspects of housetraining, it's important to be consistent in your reinforcement of your dog's behaviors. You don't need to reward him exactly the same way each time he relieves himself in the correct spot, but you do need to reward him. Carrying treats every time you go outside can be hassle, but you can always use verbal praise and petting to let your dog know that he's done a good job.

You also need to be sure that you time your rewards correctly. You want your Ridgeback to associate the reward with going to the bathroom in the right spot, rather than just going outside. If your dog thinks he gets a treat every time he goes outside, he'll go out expecting a treat rather than focusing on going to the bathroom. It can be helpful to use a verbal phrase, such as "Go potty!" to help him understand what you're asking of him. If you're using verbal praise as a reward, you can praise him immediately, but wait until he's finished before giving him a treat. Food-motivated dogs may stop

Photo Courtesy of
Kaitlyn Lamping

what they're doing in the presence of food, so it's best to wait until he's done before handing over the treats.

When taking your Rhodesian Ridgeback outside for a bathroom break, try to stay calm to keep him focused on the task at hand. The great outdoors is an interesting place that can be very exciting to a puppy. He may want to play or explore, but try to keep him focused on going to the bathroom at first. Once he's relieved himself, feel free to get excited and reward him with over-the-top praise and playtime. If he wants to explore then, that's fine. But if you let him play or explore before he relieves himself, he may get distracted and overwhelmed and forget to go at all. He may not remember that he needs to go until he comes back inside, which means you'll have a mess to clean up.

Crate Training

Although many dog owners may balk at the idea of keeping their dog in a crate while they're away from home, crates can be an incredibly effective tool in housetraining. The vast majority of dogs do not like to soil the same area that they sleep in, so crating encourages the dog to wait until she's released to relieve herself. If you allow your dog access to an entire room in your absence, she may not have a problem relieving herself in one corner and taking a nap in another. This much freedom can be detrimental your dog's housetraining progress. If she is able to relieve herself indoors without correction, but only in your absence, she'll simply learn to wait until you leave before she goes to the bathroom.

Proper crate training does not mean only crating your dog when you leave your house. If you consistently put your dog in the crate and walk out the door, he may associate his crate with your absence and begin to resist going into the crate. Instead, try to encourage your dog to relax in his crate while you're at home. Make it as comfortable as possible with blankets or bedding, provided that he does not chew or destroy anything left in the crate. You can encourage him to spend time in the crate by putting him inside while you do household chores or watch television. Once he begins to realize that the crate is somewhere to relax and it doesn't automatically mean that you're leaving, he will begin to spend time in the crate by choice. Properly crate trained dogs often choose to take their naps in their crate, simply because they feel cozy and secure inside.

Choosing an appropriately sized crate is essential to successful crate training. If you choose a crate that is too large, you may find that your dog has more accidents, simply because she has room to get away from the mess. On the other hand, if the crate is too small, your dog may feel cramped and uncomfortable and she may be unwilling to spend much time in it. A proper sized crate will give your dog enough room to stand up and turn around comfortably. She should be able to lie on her side without being too cramped. Many wire crates come with removable panels that can be placed inside the crate to adjust the size as your puppy grows. This can be more convenient than buying a new crate every time your puppy has a growth spurt.

Playpens and Doggy Doors

Playpens and doggy doors are typically not recommended during the initial stages of housetraining, simply because they give your dog too much freedom and may set him back in his training. However, as your dog progresses in his training, you may want to give him more room than his crate offers. Playpens offer more room than a crate, but not so much room that your dog can get into trouble. They can be a great intermediate step in housetraining and can be used until your dog can be trusted with more access to your house. Doggy doors are best suited for dogs who are more consistent in their housetraining. Typically, dogs will have access to an entire room or house in addition to the yard.

Before you commit to using a playpen or doggy door, you need to consider whether your Ridgeback is responsible enough to have that much freedom. If your puppy still has the occasional indoor accident, you may want to keep using the crate for a few more weeks until he's ready for the freedom of the playpen. Doggy doors also need considerable thought before you commit to purchasing one. If your dog gets into trouble outdoors, you may not want him to be able to go out whenever he pleases. He may also bring things into your house that you would prefer stayed outside. Use your best judgment and consider your dog's current stage of training before you decide to try either playpens or doggy doors.

There are many different types of playpens to choose from when shopping for your puppy. Most have panels made of wood, plastic, or wire, and the size and shape can be adjusted to suit your space. Some have gates and a few have tops or bottoms. Playpens made of lighter materials may be moved by rambunctious puppies, so be sure that your puppy can't knock over the panels or crawl under them. Some playpens also have doors or gates, so you don't have to lift your puppy in and out. Many dogs eventually learn to jump playpen panels, so it's important to keep an eye on your puppy to make sure that the playpen is still able to contain him. If he figures out how to escape, you may need to consider other options.

There are also a variety of different doggy doors available to choose from. You can find removable, temporary doors that can be placed in sliding patio doors. These doors can be removed at any time, if you choose to do so while you're away from home for extended periods of time, for example. Permanent doors can also be installed in any wall or door. Removable doors often render the sliding door unusable for humans, so consider how much use your door gets before choosing this option. These types of doors often have heavier flaps, or even two flaps, for insulation. Most doggy doors can be locked for security. If you have other pets, such as indoor-only cats, or are worried about neighborhood strays and wildlife, consider a door that locks selectively. These types of doors require your dog to wear a special tag on his collar. When the door senses the tag, it unlocks and allows the animal to come through, but if an animal approaches that isn't wearing the collar, the door remains locked. No matter which type of door you choose, make sure you pick one that is big enough to allow your Ridgeback to get through comfortably, without having to crouch or squeeze through. If the door is uncomfortable, he may be reluctant to use it.

CHAPTER 7
Socializing with People and Animals

Importance of Good Socialization

Proper socialization is important for several reasons. First, taking a well-socialized dog into new situations will put a minimal amount of stress on her. Properly socialized dogs are confident and used to encountering new people, places, and animals. Even if she's a little nervous, a well socialized dog is more likely to look to you for reassurance, rather than panic. Second, it ensures that your dog leaves a positive impression on people no matter where you take her. She will be an ambassador for the breed and even people who have never met a Rhodesian Ridgeback will fall in love with the breed. Finally, good socialization is essential to your Rhodesian Ridgeback's overall happiness because it means that she can spend more

Photo Courtesy of Stephanie Egger

time with you. She will be able to accompany you while running errands, and even to work if you work in a dog-friendly environment. You're also more likely to take a well-behaved dog with you on vacation than you are a fearful, panicky dog that overreacts to new situations. The mental stimulation your dog gets from socialization and going new places will keep her happy. Making new friends and playing with them will also keep her fit.

Good socialization is as simple as exposing your Rhodesian Ridgeback to positive experiences with new people, places, and animals. While it's best to socialize puppies while they're young, socialization can be done at any age. Use caution in any situation that you feel could overwhelm your dog or leave a negative impression on him. If a dog's first exposure to something new causes fear, he may remember that feeling and you'll then need to work on overcoming his fear, rather than progressing in his socialization. For example, dog parks might seem like a fun place to socialize your dog, but very few owners keep a close eye on their dog's body language and

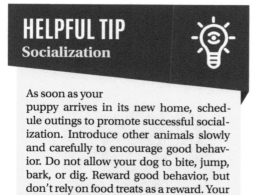

HELPFUL TIP
Socialization

As soon as your puppy arrives in its new home, schedule outings to promote successful socialization. Introduce other animals slowly and carefully to encourage good behavior. Do not allow your dog to bite, jump, bark, or dig. Reward good behavior, but don't rely on food treats as a reward. Your Ridgeback may tend toward obesity.

situations can escalate quickly. Carol Vesely of Northstar Rhodesian Ridgebacks advises, "Socialize your puppy only in controlled environments where you know the other animals and their owners." Even if your dog is not injured, even the smallest scuffle could damage your dog's confidence around strange dogs or people.

Introduce your dog to new situations slowly. Set up a few playdates with friends or family members who have dogs or children. Introduce her to one animal or person at a time and be sure to give her a little space if she seems unsure. Pushing your dog to socialize faster than she's ready can cause her to react to new situations with anxiety.

Behavior Around Other Dogs

Rhodesian Ridgebacks are confident, fun-loving dogs, but they can be wary of strange dogs if they haven't been properly socialized. Most Ridgebacks are happy to make new friends, but it's important to keep an eye on your dog's body language during all interactions with other dogs, especially if those dogs are significantly smaller. Rhodesian Ridgebacks are big dogs with powerful jaws, and they can do a lot of damage to a dog of any size, so it's crucial to prevent fights. If your dog has a tendency to display aggressive behavior around other dogs, don't be afraid to consult a professional trainer or behaviorist if necessary. The sooner aggressive behavior is corrected, the less likely your dog is to be involved in a serious fight.

When introducing two dogs, remember that a wagging tail doesn't always mean a dog is happy. Understanding canine body language is key to preventing aggressive behavior. Friendly dogs will approach each other with a relaxed posture and wagging tails. They will sniff each other with interest, but not in an intense manner. They may then go into a playful pose, or simply part ways. Unfriendly dogs will be more tense in their body language. They will hold their heads high and stiff, and although they may be wagging their tails, the rest of their body will be tense. More aggressive dogs may also growl or show their teeth. Fearful dogs may lick their lips or lower their heads in submission. They will cower and tuck their tail between their legs. If a dog is displaying fearful behavior, don't be fooled into thinking there's no chance of a fight. Fear can easily escalate into aggression, especially if the other dog pushes the fearful dog's boundaries. If your Ridgeback or the dog you are introducing to him shows anything but friendly body language, you may want to reconsider the introduction or allow the dogs more space before trying again.

Your own body language can also impact how your dog reacts during introductions. If you are fearful or stressed, you may be tensing your body or tightly gripping the leash. Your dog will sense your tension and may think that you know something he doesn't. The more relaxed you are, the more likely it is that your dog will approach other dogs as potential friends rather than possible enemies. Even if you're unsure of a situation, remain calm and confident to influence your dog to do the same.

Photo Courtesy of
Cheryl Clinton

Photo Courtesy of Adam Sexton

Ways to Socialize Your Rhodesian Ridgeback with Other Pets

Exposing your Rhodesian Ridgeback to a variety of other pets, even if he's the only animal in your home, will make him a more self-assured companion. You'll be able to take him anywhere without fear of him showing fear or aggression toward other animals. Some Rhodesian Ridgebacks have a high prey drive, so they may take more time to adjust to smaller animals such as cats. Many Ridgebacks live comfortably in multi-pet households or even farms, but it does take time and consistency for them to adapt to living safely with other animals. Remember, as sweet as your dog may be, dogs are predators and caution must be taken when introducing them to other animals. Take your time and don't push your dog or the other pet further than they are comfortable with. If either animal displays fearful or aggressive body language, discontinue the introduction immediately and give the animals some space.

Regardless of whether you are introducing your Rhodesian Ridgeback to a hamster or a horse, it's important to keep all animals restrained for their own safety. This way, if anything should go wrong, you can control the animals and separate them quickly if necessary. It can also be helpful to introduce your dog to new animals in neutral territory. Some Ridgebacks can be quite territorial, so introductions should be done in an area that is not frequented by your dog. This will also help prevent the other animal from feeling like it should defend its territory against your Ridgeback.

Until you are certain that you can predict your Ridgeback's behavior around other animals, you must never leave her unsupervised with other pets. You may need to watch your dog's interactions for several weeks or even months before you feel comfortable leaving her alone with certain animals. Some dogs may not ever be trustworthy around smaller animals such as rabbits or domestic rodents. In the case of larger animals, such as livestock, both puppies and adult dogs can be severely injured or even killed. Ridgebacks can be quite fearless and can also injure or kill animals larger than themselves if they become afraid or aggressive toward other animals. Use your best judgment to determine when and if you can trust your dog to be left alone with other animals.

Properly Greeting New People

With proper socialization Rhodesian Ridgebacks are confident and friendly dogs. However, they can be somewhat reserved around strangers if they haven't been taught that new people are potential new friends. Teaching your Ridgeback to properly greet strangers is key to making progress toward having a well-socialized dog. If you have a timid puppy or an adult who hasn't been socialized much, you may need to introduce strangers slowly and methodically. Some dogs may be particularly afraid of men or children and may need extra time dedicated to those types of introductions. It's important to introduce your dog to as many different types of people as possible to get him used to the realities of life among humans. The bigger the variety of people you can introduce to your dog, the less likely he is to have a negative reaction toward strangers and the more confident he will be while accompanying you in your daily life.

The best way to introduce your dog to new people is to allow her to approach them on her own. Shoving her toward strangers or pulling her toward them on a leash is likely to create tension and anxiety, setting the introduction up for failure. If your Ridgeback seems uncomfortable, ask the new people to let her sniff them for a bit before they try to pet her. Reaching out toward a fearful dog can cause her to lash out to try and defend herself. If your dog is on the other end of the spectrum and is quite enthusiastic about meeting new people, you may need to work on keeping her calm. Most people don't enjoy having dogs jump on their laps and lick their face in greeting, so you need to teach your dog to greet people calmly and respectfully. Keeping your dog on a leash during introductions will help you control her. Ask your dog to sit politely before allowing the new people to pet her. It may take a few repetitions for your dog to learn that she must sit quietly before she can say hello, but eventually she will learn that she can only get the attention of new people by patiently waiting for them to greet her first.

If your dog seems fearful when meeting new people, it's crucial that you do not comfort him during this time. Comforting a fearful dog will not give him confidence, it will only reassure him that he needs to be worried about the situation. Instead, you may need to correct him for growling or barking. You can also try to distract your dog by asking him to sit or focus on you. You can have the new person offer him treats to encourage him to approach. Remember to use plenty of positive reinforcement when your Ridgeback behaves appropriately.

Rhodesian Ridgebacks and Children

Children and dogs can be ideal companions, but a lot of preparation and supervision must be dedicated to their interaction in the beginning to ensure a safe and friendly relationship. Rhodesian Ridgebacks are large dogs and can easily knock over or accidently injure a child, especially a toddler. Care must also be taken to educate children on the proper way to interact with dogs. Some dogs do not respond well to roughhousing or heavy-handed affection, so supervision is essential to keep everyone safe and comfortable.

Prior to introducing your Rhodesian Ridgeback to your children, you need to have a conversation with the kids about the proper way to handle a dog. If you wait until the actual introduction to have this discussion, you may find that the kids are too overwhelmed by the presence of the adorable dog to listen to you. Younger children may not understand that they are hurting the dog by tugging on his ears or tail and the dog may respond with fear or aggression. You must explain to the kids that they should be gentle with the dog and treat him with respect. They should not try to climb on adult dogs or try to pick up puppies. Once you are confident that they understand the rules of interacting with a dog, then you can introduce them to their new family member.

Kids and puppies can be easily overwhelmed with the excitement of the first introduction, so it's important that you go slowly and supervise the interaction closely. Be prepared to correct the behavior of both the children and the dog if necessary. If things get out of control, you can always ask everyone to take a break and try again later. You may need to do several short sessions before everyone is calm enough to interact responsibly. Be sure to use plenty of positive reinforcement and praise both the children and the dog when they play calmly and appropriately. If your dog displays any signs of fear, you may need to have the children try to hand him a few treats to encourage him to interact.

Under no circumstances should you leave your children and your new dog unattended during the first few weeks or even months together. Accidents can happen in the blink of an eye and only proper supervision can prevent a tragedy. Most of the time, injuries are purely accidental, but the more excited and rambunctious everyone gets, the more likely it is that it will end in injury. To prevent the kids or dog from getting hurt, it's best to keep an eye on everyone until you can trust that they can play together safely.

CHAPTER 8
Rhodesian Ridgebacks and Your Other Pets

Introducing Your New Puppy to Other Animals

HELPFUL TIP
Careful Now!

Because your Ridgeback is a hunting dog, it may be prone to aggression with other animals. It was bred to pursue and seize lions in Africa, and it may grab and injure cats or other small animals. Male Rhodesian Ridgebacks can sometimes be dominant and aggressive toward other male dogs. Use caution when introducing your dog to other males.

When you first introduce your new Rhodesian Ridgeback puppy to other animals, you need to make sure you dedicate plenty of time to the process and don't rush the interaction. Your puppy or the other animal may show signs of discomfort or anxiety at first, so try letting them view or smell each other from a distance. As they get used to each other, you can decrease the distance between them until they are meeting face to face. However, only allow the animals to get as close as they are comfortable with. Rushing the introduction may frighten either your puppy or the other animal and it will then require more time and work on your part to get them used to each other.

Restraint is one of the most important safety aspects of any introduction. Your puppy needs to be restrained in order to keep her under control as well as to be able to pull her out of a situation should it go wrong. The same applies to the other animal, no matter what species you're introducing your puppy to. It can be helpful to keep a fence between your puppy and large animals. This way, neither animal can get out of hand and injure the other.

Proper supervision is essential to any introduction. Until you know how your puppy will react to other animals and how the other animals will respond to your puppy, you shouldn't leave them alone together for even a moment until you are confident that nothing will go wrong.

Pack Mentality

Dogs are pack animals and as such, they prefer to have a structured hierarchy in their family group. Dogs are social animals that find comfort in the rules and limitations set by the leader of their group. Most dogs prefer to be followers, rather than leaders, but some dogs are more dominant and will try to take charge more often than their more submissive counterparts. Dominant dogs will attempt to challenge you as leader much more frequently than submissive dogs, so keep in mind that your dog's individual personality will affect how easily he accepts his position in your pack. Whether you have one dog or ten, you need to make it clear that you are the leader of the pack. A dog without rules or limitations can be dangerous. Rhodesian Ridgebacks in particular can be a danger to themselves and others if they are allowed to rule the household.

Photo Courtesy of Stephanie Egger

Photo Courtesy of Jamie Zimmermann

It can be easy to let your adorable new puppy get away with certain behaviors, but you need to keep in mind that your dog may weigh up to 90 pounds as an adult. Naughty or exuberant behavior is not nearly as cute when your dog is big enough to knock over or injure you. Actions such as growling at strangers, resource guarding, or refusing to move from the sofa when asked are all behaviors that can escalate into more serious problems if not corrected. If you can get your Ridgeback's behavior under control while she's still young, it will be much easier to correct than when she's a full-grown adult. Don't be afraid to consult a trainer or behaviorist if you begin to struggle with your dog's dominant behavior. It's better to seek help early on before the behavior escalates.

In a dog's natural pack setting, the leader is allowed to do as he pleases. He eats first, sleeps where he likes, and never has to move out of the way of other dogs. As the pack leader in your home, you must behave similarly to a dog's leader in the wild in order to maintain your position. You need to set boundaries and enforce them consistently. Never kick, hit, or yell at your dog to correct him. He is more likely to become afraid and confused than to understand that he's done something wrong. Instead, teach your dog the meaning of the word 'no' and use confident body language. If you ask your dog to move off the couch and he doesn't respond, you need to move him out of the way. Ask your dog to sit and wait politely for his food at mealtimes. You can even set the food down in front him and ask him to wait for your signal before he is allowed to eat. You must also never allow your Ridgeback to rush through a doorway in front of you. In a natural pack setting, dogs rely on this social order to maintain a calm and stable pack. Your home and family should reflect this, so be sure that all human members of your family consistently reinforce their position in the pack. Even children can be calm, assertive pack leaders, so make sure that your kids understand the rules too.

Fighting/Bad Behavior

Aggressive behavior should be corrected at the first sign. If your Rhodesian Ridgeback is allowed to display aggressive behavior, it will escalate until it turns into an actual fight. It may start with your puppy growling at another dog for approaching a food bowl or toy. If you don't correct this seemingly small action, your dog may feel comfortable snapping at the other dog the next time. Rhodesian Ridgebacks are large dogs with powerful jaws and even a quick bite can be enough to seriously injure or even kill another dog, especially if it is significantly smaller. Aggression does not start with an all-out fight; it will start small and build up to violence. Aggressive behavior must be dealt with immediately, so if you do not feel that you can deal with your dog's behavior on your own, you need to seek out professional help.

If you see your puppy begin to engage in aggressive behavior or he starts to bully another dog, you can correct his behavior with a loud clap, stomp, or sharp "No!" This will startle your Ridgeback and distract him before his behavior can escalate. You can continue to distract him by asking him to sit or lie down. Making him focus on you instead of the other dog will help diffuse the tension and hopefully prevent a fight.

The key to preventing a dog fight is to determine what is triggering your dog's aggressive behavior in the first place. If you can't figure out why your dog is acting out, you'll never be able to completely solve the problem. If you notice that your dog only becomes aggressive when another dog approaches her toys or food bowl, you know you're dealing with resource guarding and can use that information to form a plan such as separating the dogs to feed them.

If your dog does get into an actual fight, use extreme caution when attempting to break up the fight. Never grab a dog in a fight with your bare hands. A fighting dog will often turn around and bite you without taking the time to consider his actions. He won't recognize that it's you in this heightened state of mind. Depending on the intensity of the fight, you may be able to break it up with a loud noise. Clapping, stomping, or banging food bowls together works well. This is the one time that it is appropriate to yell at your dog. Spraying or splashing the dogs with water can also be an effective method of breaking up a fight. Water won't hurt the dogs, but it will be surprising enough that it may stop them from fighting. If you absolutely must intervene physically, decide which dog is the aggressor and grab that dog by the hind legs. Once you have the dog's legs, pull him away from the other dog quickly. If you don't do this quickly enough, he may be able to turn around and bite you. Once you have the dogs separated, quickly restrain or separate them before they can begin fighting again.

Raising Multiple Puppies from the Same Litter

Raising your Rhodesian Ridgeback alongside a littermate might seem like an appealing idea, especially if you have no other pets in the home. Your puppy might be more comfortable moving into a new household if he has a brother or sister to keep him company. You won't have to worry about introducing him to an older dog who might be resistant to change. You also won't need to worry about leaving your puppy home alone, knowing that he has someone to keep him company. You will also spend less time exercising your puppy because he'll have a playmate 24/7.

Photo Courtesy of Steve Warwick

However, there are many drawbacks to raising multiple puppies from the same litter. More puppies mean more mess. You'll also need to dedicate more time to supervising and training. Dogs who have been bonded since birth make for great friends, but if you ever need to separate them it can be a problem. If you need to take one to the vet, for instance, you may find that they panic or experience separation anxiety when apart. They may also be more fearful or insecure when they're on their own since they usually have their littermate at their side to boost their confidence. Another concern is that if your Ridgebacks develop bad habits for any reason, you'll have multiple dogs that could potentially develop the habit and it can be significantly more difficult to break bad habits in multiple dogs.

The biggest concerns when considering whether you should bring home multiple dogs are time and money. You need to carefully consider how much you are willing to commit to your dogs. If you have other obligations in your life, such as work and family, raising a single puppy may be difficult enough as it is. Housetraining can be an especially time-consuming process with multiple puppies.

If you do decide to adopt littermates, most experts recommend training the puppies together and apart. Training them together will help you gain control over them when you need to walk them together, for instance. It will teach them to behave well as a unit and will help boost their confidence in new situations. However, you also need to spend plenty of time training them separately to prevent separation anxiety and give them more confidence when they are out with you on their own.

Another option you may want to consider is adopting one Rhodesian Ridgeback now and another at a later date. This gives you the chance to get one dog settled into your home and your daily routine before introducing another. You'll be able to get a start on the first dog's training and won't need to work on two completely untrained dogs at the same time. Having a slightly older dog in the family will also give the second dog a role model. He can look to his older companion for reassurance in new situations. Adopting dogs at different times will also give you the chance to seriously consider whether you are willing to take on the responsibility of multiple dogs.

Options if Your Pets Don't Get Along

Some pets need more time to adjust to a new companion than others, so if your existing pets don't get along with your Rhodesian Ridgeback right away, don't worry quite yet. Don't rush your introductions and don't make any serious decisions about the situation until you've given your pets adequate time to adjust to their new living arrangements. It can take several weeks, or even months, before your pets can be trusted to safely be left alone together. In the beginning, you may need to limit the amount of time your existing pets spend with your new puppy. If you have much older dogs, Sandra Fikes of Kalahari Rhodesian Ridgebacks suggests, "Never allow puppies to harass old dogs. It's not fair to them, so when the older one has had enough, give them a way out or remove the puppy to another activity." Sharing space and affection can be difficult for some pets and they may simply need more time to get used to the situation.

It can be distressing to consider giving up a beloved pet in the event that your pets do not get along. If this isn't something you're willing to consider, you need to develop a plan to minimize the interactions of your pets. You may have to do this for the rest of their lives, so you need to carefully consider whether you are willing to dedicate that much time and effort.

You'll need to make sure that each pet has separate but equal space and that you give each of them the same amount of time and affection. It can be exhausting to manage two or more pets in the same household while keeping them separated, so before you make this decision, think about whether you are willing to provide that level of care for them and if it's really the best decision for their happiness and well-being.

If you do decide that you can't manage your pets separately in your home for the rest of their lives, you will need to find another home for one of your pets. Many pets simply do better in a single-pet household, while others just need a different environment. It can be a heartbreaking decision to give up a beloved pet, but as a pet owner it's your responsibility to make the best decisions for your animals. The happiness and well-being of all of your pets should be your priority.

CHAPTER 9
Physical and Mental Exercise

Exercise Requirements

One look at a Rhodesian Ridgeback will tell you that the breed is capable of incredible athletic endeavors. However, despite their fit appearance, they do not need hours of physical exercise in order to behave themselves in your home. That said, physical and mental exercise are crucial to your dog's overall health. Dogs who do not receive enough physical activity are prone to weight gain and weight-related health conditions.

Carol Vesely of Northstar Rhodesian Ridgebacks says, "They don't need to run 10 miles every day. A couple mile walk each day and some training classes to stimulate them mentally and they will be very easy to manage around the house." Of course, if you run 10 miles every day, your Rhodesian Ridgeback will happily keep you company. Well-exercised dogs are also more likely to focus on you during training sessions, both at home and around town.

Photo Courtesy of Stephanie Egger

The exact amount of exercise your dog needs will depend on a few factors. Your Ridgeback's age, energy level, and overall health will impact how much daily exercise he needs to stay fit and happy. Most experts recommend between 30 minutes and two hours of activity each day. This time may include walking, hiking, jogging, playing, or participating in dog sports such as agility or obedience. For young puppies, it's best to spread this time out over several sessions throughout the day. Too much physical activity at one time can permanently damage growing joints, so try to keep your dog busy with several 15-minute sessions of work or play throughout the day. As your dog matures, you can increase the length of each exercise or training session. Ideally, you should give your dog the opportunity to exercise twice per day, especially if you're away from your home for long periods of time during the day. A tired dog is more likely to rest patiently while you're at work and settle down for bedtime in the evening.

HELPFUL TIP
Get Physical

Your Ridgeback is a muscular animal that needs regular, vigorous exercise to maintain its health. Play fetch with your dog often, and add swimming to its routine if possible. This breed is a good running partner, but always keep your dog on a leash. Regular training and a firm set of rules will encourage a healthy, happy companion.

No matter how much physical exercise your Rhodesian Ridgeback gets, you must be able to mentally stimulate her on a regular basis as well. Mental exercise is especially important for older dogs or those with physical limitations. Just because their bodies can't keep up anymore, doesn't mean their minds don't need regular stimulation. To stave off boredom, try holding several short training sessions throughout the day. For young puppies, keep the sessions short, no more than five minutes or so. For adult dogs, sessions of about 15 to 20 minutes at a time are ideal. Any longer than this and your dog may lose focus. Mental exercise can be quite exhausting so you may find that your dog gets tired more quickly when she has to use her mind. You may also want to try various puzzle or treat toys designed to keep your dog's mind engaged while you accomplish other tasks. Getting involved in dog sports, such as agility or lure coursing, is a great way to exercise your Rhodesian Ridgeback's mind and body.

Different Types of Exercise to Try

Photo Courtesy of Cheryl Clinton

Rhodesian Ridgebacks are natural athletes that excel in many different types of dog sports. If you've never competed in dog sports before, you may want to consider trying out a few to see which ones you and your dog prefer. Training and competing with your dog will not only keep you both physically and mentally fit, but the time you spend together will strengthen your bond and improve your relationship.

One of the most popular sports for dog owners of all breeds to compete in is obedience. The sport requires handlers to walk or jog through a course and perform a variety of tasks such as sit, stay, or down. There are different levels of difficulty for dogs and handlers. In the lower levels, the tasks are simpler, and they are performed with the dog on a leash. At more advanced levels, the tasks become more difficult and are done off-leash. Rally obedience is also rising in popularity and tends to be faster paced than traditional obedience. The course of 10-20 tasks is marked out by signs and handlers and dogs must work together to complete the course quickly and accurately.

Dock diving is a fun and interesting new sport that is ideal for water-loving dogs. Dogs compete by jumping into a pool of water one at a time after a floating toy. Dock diving is not a sport that relies on a dog's speed, but rather his strength and jumping ability. A toy is hung above a pool of water in front of a platform. When the handler releases the dog, the dog is able to get a running start and then jump out over the water in order to grab the toy. The dog that jumps the farthest wins the competition.

Flyball is an exciting and fast-paced sport ideal for athletic breeds like the Rhodesian Ridgeback. Dogs compete as a team, racing over hurdles one at a time to pounce on a box that releases a tennis ball. The dogs catch the ball, then race back to the starting point and once they cross the line, the next dog is released. This is a timed event and the fastest team wins, so speed and agility are essential.

Lure coursing is a popular sport among Rhodesian Ridgeback owners because of the breed's natural prey drive. Lure coursing gives your dog the opportunity to feel the thrill of chasing down prey, but in a safe and controlled environment. The "prey" is a mechanical plastic lure that is pulled around a course in a zigzag pattern that represents the natural path of a fleeing rabbit or squirrel. The AKC only allows certain types of hounds to compete in the sport, and Rhodesian Ridgebacks are on the list.

If you're looking to stay fit alongside your dog, you may consider trying Canicross. Canicross is a relatively new sport, popular in Europe, that is gaining popularity in North America, as well. Fast, athletic breeds such as the Rhodesian Ridgeback excel in Canicross. Dogs wear harnesses, similar to those of sled dogs, that are attached to a bungee leash. The leash is then attached either to a handler's bicycle or a harness worn around the handler's waist. The dog then runs for a specified distance, pulling the handler on either his or her feet or a bicycle. Distances and terrain may vary from race to race, but Canicross is a challenging and fun way to stay fit and bond with your dog.

Photo Courtesy of
Nicola King

Photo Courtesy of Andrea Gorog

Importance of Mental Exercise

Keeping your Rhodesian Ridgeback's mind active is crucial to keeping him focused on his training and out of trouble. Without enough mental exercise, your Ridgeback may seek to entertain himself by developing rude and destructive behaviors. Once a dog experiences the inherent reward of getting into the trash can or escaping the yard, it can take weeks or even months of firm and consistent training to break the habit. Rather than having to fix the problem, many bad habits can be prevented by providing your dog with safe and appropriate ways to entertain himself. Often, mental stimulation will wear a dog out in a much shorter period of time than physical exercise would. Many dogs need a break after just 15 to 20 minutes of intense focus.

Mental stimulation is especially important to dogs with physical limitations. Young puppies, for instance, should not be exercised strenuously until their growth plates have closed, usually at around 18 months of age or so. Many senior dogs are limited by conditions such as arthritis or a lack of fitness. Dogs with physical limitations usually do not have any mental limitations, so keeping them busy in a way that doesn't stress their body is crucial. Puzzle toys or sports like scent work or obedience are great ways to work your dog's mind without putting too much strain on their bodies. Dogs are capable of learning new tricks and tasks at any age, so don't be afraid to teach your senior dog something new.

As stated earlier, mental stimulation can often tire a dog out much faster than physical stimulation. Dogs who are physically capable of running for hours may need a break after just 15 minutes of intense training, so try to keep your sessions short. Younger dogs may need even shorter training sessions, usually no more than five minutes or so. If you keep training past your dog's point of exhaustion, he may become unfocused and unmotivated when you begin the next session. If you notice your dog tiring at around 15 minutes, you may want to try quitting at around 12 or 13 minutes, before he loses focus. This way, you'll be able to end on a good note and he'll be more engaged in your next session.

Tips for Keeping Your Rhodesian Ridgeback Occupied

Since many Rhodesian Ridgebacks are food-motivated, hiding food in interesting places is one of the best ways to keep your dog busy until you can provide proper supervision. If you're worried about the extra calories, you can always use a small portion of your dog's daily kibble in these activities. Some owners even opt to give their dogs their entire meals using puzzle toys, just to keep them busy for longer periods of time. Keep a close eye on your dog's waistline and use your best judgment to determine whether you should use extra treats or a portion of kibble to entertain your dog.

Your local pet store or favorite online retailer likely has a selection of wooden or plastic puzzle toys. These toys can be stuffed with small treats or pieces of kibble and your dog must work to get the food out. Puzzle toys usually have a variety of flaps, cups, knobs, or sliding doors that your dog must navigate in order to reach the food. They also come in different levels of difficulty, so as your dog learns how to solve the puzzle, you can always increase the challenge with a new toy. Many owners opt to have several different types of puzzle toys that they rotate on a regular basis to keep their Ridgebacks stimulated and challenged. Puzzle toys are a great way to keep your dog out of trouble while you focus on household chores or work.

Photo Courtesy of
Liesl Kruger

Stuffable rubber chew toys, such as Kongs, are also a great way to prevent your Rhodesian Ridgeback from getting into trouble. Like puzzle toys, they can be stuffed with food to keep your dog interested and challenged for long periods of time. These types of toys usually have a hollow center that can be stuffed with any type of food or treat. They also come in a variety of sizes and densities, so if you have a young puppy or an elderly dog with dental problems, you can find an appropriate toy. Some dogs learn rather quickly how to hold the toy to reach the treats inside, so don't be afraid to use foods that are more difficult to get out. Kibble is a popular choice, but many owners use canned dog food, small amounts of peanut butter, or even vegetables to stuff into the center of the toy. On particularly warm days, or to increase the challenge, you can even freeze the toy to make it last longer and provide refreshment. It's not uncommon for dog owners to have several stuffed Kongs in the freezer, ready to take out at a moment's notice.

Snuffle mats are a new and interesting way of providing dogs with mental stimulation. They are flat mats made of easy-to-clean material such as fleece. Similar in appearance to a shag rug, the mats are covered in long strips of fabric. They can be purchased online, or made at home using simple instructions found on the internet. To use, simply sprinkle a handful of kibble or small treats across the rug. Before giving the mat to your dog, you can ruffle up the fabric strips to distribute the treats deeper. Hiding treats in this manner requires your dog to use his sense of smell to seek out the treats and simulates your dog's natural instinct to forage for food. Snuffle mats are ideal for dogs of any age, especially those suffering from physical limitations, since the mat can even be used by dogs lying down.

CHAPTER 10
Training Your Rhodesian Ridgeback

Clear Expectations

During your training sessions with your Rhodesian Ridgeback, it's important for you to have clear expectations of yourself. Remember, without clear and consistent communication, no progress can be made. Unless you're willing to dedicate a significant amount of time and work to your dog's training, you may end up disappointed with your dog's progress. If you only work with your dog once or twice per week, you're not going to see the progress in your Ridgeback's training that you would if you were training her every single day. It's also going to be more difficult for your dog to remember what you asked of her in the last session if you only work with her infrequently. This will result in you both becoming frustrated and losing focus. Instead, set small, manageable goals for yourself and your dog. If you can only manage a few minutes of training in the evenings after you come home from work, then schedule that training session every day, even if it's only ten minutes. Your dog is going to get more out of a daily ten-minute session than she would a once weekly 30-minute training session.

Photo Courtesy of
Joanne Baker

When working with your Ridgeback, you must also have reasonable expectations of him and where he is in his training. Do not ask more of your dog than he is capable of at a particular stage of his training. For example, if you're able to get him to sit quietly and focus on you while inside your home, but he loses focus in your yard about half the time, you can't expect to take him to the local dog park and have him listen to you. Expecting more of your dog than he can handle is unfair. You must always be willing to set your dog up for success. Training must be done in small steps, progressing only when you're confident that your dog can handle it. If you know your dog will make a mistake or react badly to a situation, it's best to avoid that situation if possible until you are certain he is trained enough to handle it.

No matter how your training session goes, it's important for you to always end the session on a good note. Even if your dog is struggling with a certain concept or is getting tired and losing focus, you must try to end the session with positivity. Ending with frustration or negativity will only set your dog up for failure during the next session. You want her to look forward to training. If your dog is getting tired or doesn't seem to understand what you're asking of her, go back to something she's good at. Ask her to sit or lie down a few times. Even if the task is simple, you will be able to reward her for performing the command. After a few successful repetitions, you can end the session and try the more difficult task again later.

Operant Conditioning Basics

Photo Courtesy of Beth Keener

Operant conditioning is a type of learning that is based on the idea that behavior can be shaped based on the environmental response to the behavior, whether it is a reward or a punishment. Renowned American psychologist and behaviorist B.F. Skinner was one of the first to promote the idea. Skinner did not believe that animals and humans learn solely through classical conditioning, as he believed that we are too complex to learn only through such a simple method. He hypothesized that behaviors followed by an enjoyable, positive experience are more likely to be repeated than behaviors followed by unpleasant or negative experiences. Skinner referred to these environmental responses as operants. Skinner theorized that there are three types of operants: neutral operants, reinforcers, and punishments. Neutral operants do not increase or decrease the likelihood of the behavior being repeated in the future. The environmental response is not positive or negative enough to affect future behavior. Reinforcers, which can be positive or negative, increase the likelihood of a certain behavior being repeated in the future. Punishments are always negative and will discourage the behavior from being performed again.

One of the most popular and successful methods of dog training is positive reinforcement. Positive reinforcement uses the idea of Skinner's reinforcer operant to encourage a dog to perform a behavior on command. Generally, dogs are rewarded using praise, food, or toys. Carol Vesely of Northstar Rhodesian Ridgebacks says, "Ridgebacks are very food motivated and will generally work well for food." Unfortunately, positive reinforcement can also work against you in the development of bad habits. For example, if your Ridgeback bolts out the front door and is reward with an off-leash romp through the neighborhood and a good game of chase, he's more likely to repeat the behavior in the future. Preventing bad habits from developing can only be accomplished by managing both your dog's behavior and the environmental responses to his actions.

HELPFUL TIP
Willful Companion

Rhodesian Ridgebacks can be stubborn and strong-willed. Owners are advised to give firm, clear, and consistent commands. If you are unable to put in the amount of time necessary to train your Ridgeback, you might consider a professional trainer who is familiar with the breed.

Negative reinforcement is another method of dog training, often used in combination with positive reinforcement. Negative reinforcement should not be confused with punishment, as it encourages a behavior to be repeated. This method works to reward the dog with the removal of an unpleasant sensation. To combine this negative reinforcement with positive reinforcement, you may simultaneously remove the pressure or unpleasant sensation and reward your dog with treats or verbal praise.

Punishment differs from negative reinforcement in that it discourages the dog from repeating the behavior in the future. For example, if you catch your Rhodesian Ridgeback in the act of attempting to dig a hole beneath your fence, you may disrupt his behavior with a loud clap, stomp, or "No!" If his attempts to dig a hole are always met with an unpleasant and startling noise, he's less likely to attempt the behavior again in the future. However, the punishment a dog receives should never be too harsh. Serious behaviors such as fighting obviously deserve a harsher punishment, such as being sprayed with water, whereas that would too harsh of a punishment for digging a hole in the yard. If your punishments are too severe, you may find that they do not correct the bad behavior and instead result in fearful or aggressive reactions. Punishments should be used as little as possible and should never involve hurting your dog. Under no circumstances should you hit or kick your dog. Usually, a simple but loud clap or stomp, or at most a spray of water, should be sufficient.

Primary Reinforcements—Food, Toys, Playtime

Primary reinforcements typically stem from rewards that are biological in nature. This can include the use of food, toys, and playtime in training. Dogs naturally find food rewarding and will readily repeat behaviors that are followed with treats. Toys and playtime are used less frequently, but still reward the dog on a biological level. Play works as a reward by imitating a dog's natural behavior. Dogs naturally find the thrill of chasing down and catching their prey rewarding, so it's possible to simulate this behavior as a reward using a toy and a game of fetch or tug. Dogs with particularly high prey drives often find this type of reinforcement to be particularly reward-ing. For Rhodesian Ridgebacks, some dogs may be more motivated by food, while others find play to be more valuable. Carol Vesely of Northstar Rhode-sian Ridgebacks says, "It is not in their nature to automatically do what their owners ask of them, so you need to make it motivating for them to want to please you. Find what motivates your dog and use that as their reward."

Most dogs are naturally food-motivated to some degree, so it's one of the most popular ways to reward a dog for good behavior. Biologically, dogs need to food to survive, but more importantly, they just really enjoy eating. As with humans, it's not uncommon for dogs to prefer certain foods over others, so you may need to try out a few different types of food to deter-mine which ones your dog deems high value. Some dogs will work only for their favorite treat, while others are happy performing for a portion of their daily kibble.

For some dogs, their prey drive outweighs their motivation for food. For this type of dog, rewarding them with a toy or playtime may work better than food. Dogs with low prey drives may need some encouragement be-fore they come to enjoy this type of reinforcement, or it may not work at all. The key to using play as a reward is to make it as exciting as possible. Hand-ing your dog a squeaky toy is not exciting and it will not work as a reward. Toys that can be thrown or tugged on are ideal. Allowing your dog to jump or chase after the toy will trigger his natural instinct to give chase. Some dogs also thrive on vigorous games of tug-of-war. Whatever type of play your dog enjoys most, be sure to exaggerate your own excitement. If he sees how happy you are, he'll get more enjoyment out of the reward than if you simply tossed his favorite ball across the yard.

Secondary Reinforcements—Attention, Praise, Clickers

Secondary reinforcements can also be considered learned reinforcements. Most dogs do not naturally find praise or attention rewarding, and the sound of a clicker means nothing to an untrained dog. They learn the value of these types of rewards through association with primary reinforcements. In the beginning, it can be helpful to combine secondary reinforcements with primary reinforcements until your dog learns the value of rewards such as praise or a marker noise such as the clicker.

Photo Courtesy of
Heather Proper-VanValkenberg

Attention and praise work well as a reward for many dogs without having to build the connection with primary reinforcements. However, not all dogs respond well to praise on its own. Deciding on a marker word, such as "good" or "yes" and using the same word consistently will help your dog understand the value of verbal praise. Be sure to say the word in a positive and upbeat way. Your tone and body language will speak more to your dog than your words in the beginning. Using verbal praise and even physical attention in connection to primary reinforcements will increase the value of these rewards so that eventually your dog will understand that she's done the right thing when you say the marker word, even if she doesn't get a treat.

Clicker training is similar to using a marker word, but instead of a verbal cue, you're using a specific sound to reward the dog. Dogs will not immediately understand the value of the noise so you'll need to build that association. Most trainers recommend focusing solely on building this connection before moving on in your dog's training. For example, if you want to use the clicker as a secondary reinforcement, the first few training sessions should consist of you pressing the clicker and handing her a treat. After a few repetitions, your dog will learn that the click is associated with a treat. As you progress in your training, you can continue to combine the two reinforcements until your dog learns that performing the correct behavior will result in either a primary or secondary reinforcement.

Negative Reinforcement

Negative reinforcement should not be confused with punishment. Punishment is when a behavior is followed by an unpleasant experience, such as a loud noise. Punishments are used to discourage a dog from repeating certain behaviors. Negative reinforcement differs in that it actually encourages a dog to repeat a behavior. As previously mentioned, negative reinforcement works by rewarding a dog with the removal of an unpleasant sensation, such as pressure on the leash. When used correctly, it can be a valuable tool for training, especially when combined with positive reinforcement.

An example of negative reinforcement can be found in traditional leash training. Most dogs will not naturally give in to leash pressure. Instead, they will brace against it and pull in the opposite direction of the leash. Negative reinforcement can be used to teach a dog polite leash manners by teaching the dog that the pressure of the leash will be released when he takes a

*Photo Courtesy of
Rebecca Weddell*

step toward the pressure. By putting gentle pressure on the leash and immediately releasing that pressure the moment the dog steps forward, you are teaching him that the way he can relieve the discomfort of the leash is to give in to it. When combined with positive reinforcement, such as a treat or praise, your dog will quickly learn to walk in the direction that you are telling him to go.

Caution must be used when training with negative reinforcement because if you put too much pressure or do not release at the right moment, your dog can become fearful and develop aversive behaviors. Your timing on the release of pressure must be exact. If you do not release the moment your dog performs the correct behavior, he will not make the connection with his behavior and the removal of the pressure. You must also be aware of how much pressure you are putting on your dog. It should be enough to be mildly unpleasant, but never painful. Putting more pressure on your dog than he is comfortable with will result in fear, rather than learning. Negative reinforcement is best used in combination with positive reinforcement. If you have any doubts about your abilities to use negative reinforcement correctly, consult a professional trainer or simply use positive reinforcement on its own.

Hiring a Trainer/Attending Classes

Although some Rhodesian Ridgeback owners train their dogs successfully without the assistance of a professional, many find that hiring a trainer or attending training classes helps them accomplish their goals faster and with fewer problems. Even lifelong dog owners can benefit from the professional advice of a trainer or behaviorist.

With most trainers, you'll have the option of either private lessons or group classes. Both types of class have their advantages, so you need to consider your dog's current stage of training as well as your end goals before deciding which one is best for you. In private lessons, you have the benefit of the trainer's undivided attention. This can be particularly helpful if you're struggling with aggression or behavioral problems. In some cases, you may want to start with private lessons and progress to group lessons as you and your dog become more confident. In group lessons, you are able to work on training your dog with distractions. He'll have to learn to focus on you with other dogs and handlers around. This will help prepare you both for the distractions of the real world. Group classes are also usually much cheaper than private lessons.

If you are struggling to get to your dog to understand what you are asking, or you believe your dog is developing bad habits or behavioral issues, you should definitely consider seeking professional advice. There's no shame in asking for help and it's better to start working on a solution to your problems before they escalate into more serious or dangerous behavior. Remember, trainers work with difficult dogs on a daily basis, so they are capable of handling a vast variety of different personalities and behaviors. The sooner you seek help, the sooner you and your dog can start working together rather than against each other.

Owner Behavior

One of the most important and often overlooked aspects of dog training is the handler's behavior. You must be willing to hold yourself accountable for your actions and how they affect your dog. If you aren't completely dedicated to your dog's training, it's likely that she will recognize this and react accordingly. She may try to bully you or simply ignore your commands. You must approach each training session with consistency, firmness, and enthusiasm.

If you are having difficulties in your dog's training, it may be helpful to reflect on your own behavior and whether you may be causing the problem, at least in part. Dogs are aware of even the subtlest changes in body language, so you may be sending the wrong message without even realizing it. Having the willingness to reflect on your own behavior and body language and working to improve yourself will help you become a more effective trainer.

If you've reflected on your own behavior and have identified a number of reasons for your training struggles, it may be a good idea to get a second opinion. Having another set of eyes on you during training sessions may help you determine the source of your problems. If you have dog-savvy friends or family members, ask them to watch one of your training sessions. You can even seek professional advice if you feel that a trainer or behaviorist is best suited for the situation. No matter how skilled of a trainer you are, it doesn't hurt to get a second opinion. Another person may be able to see something that you've simply missed or are unaware of.

CHAPTER 11
Basic Commands

Benefits of Proper Training

HELPFUL TIP
Provide a Set Schedule

The commands of "Speak" and "Quiet" are helpful to teach simultaneously. Use clear hand signals along with vocal commands when training your Ridgeback. Be cautious when using food treats, as your dog may become dependent on them. As with all large breeds, "Sit," "Down," and "Stay" are best taught early.

One of the greatest benefits to training sessions with your Rhodesian Ridgeback is the mental stimulation it provides. Even if you only work with him for 5-10 minutes at a time, you're still making him use his brain. Depending on the type of training session, you may also be exercising his body, which will help keep him fit and healthy. Training sessions with your Ridgeback will also strengthen your bond and increase the trust between you.

Additionally, a properly trained Rhodesian Ridgeback will be able to go anywhere with you. Along with socialization, training can help give your dog the confidence to handle himself responsibly no matter what you encounter on your adventures together. Whether you're traveling on summer vacation or simply strolling through the neighborhood, you can trust that your dog will be able to handle himself with confidence and grace. This will also leave a positive impression on the people you meet. Your dog can become an ambassador for his breed, impressing people with his good behavior. The more that you are able to take your dog out and about with you, the happier he will be. He'll be mentally stimulated by the new experiences and he'll be happy that he can spend more time with the people he loves.

Proper training is also crucial to you and your Ridgeback's safety. A well-trained dog is unlikely to run out into traffic or get into a fight with another dog. You'll be able to trust your dog no matter where you take him. You can also trust your dog not to hurt you. Teaching him proper leash manners means he's less likely to pull you to the ground if he sees a squirrel on your walk. Along with regular training sessions, you must also constantly remind your dog that you are the leader of the pack.

Photo Courtesy of
Linda Hafer

Different Training Methods

If you speak to ten different dog trainers about their preferred methods, you will probably walk away with ten different opinions. There are many different training methods, and each trainer likely does things a little bit different from the next. Trainers who specialize in certain sports may also have different ways of teaching their dogs. The personality and preferences of the individual dog will also dictate which type of training is necessary. Some dogs do best using strictly positive reinforcement, while others need a bit of negative reinforcement as well. There may be some trial and error in finding what training method works best for you and your dog, so don't be afraid to try a few out or seek the opinion of a few trainers. Most importantly, do what's best for your individual dog.

Basic Commands

The sky is the limit when it comes to teaching your dog new commands. Depending on your long-term goals for your Rhodesian Ridgeback, you may need to eventually teach her sport-specific commands, but there are a number of commands that every dog should know, regardless of whether she's competing or keeping you company at home. Every dog should know commands such as sit, stay, and come. Teaching your dog to get off the furniture when asked or give up her toy or chew treat is also essential to maintaining a balanced pack within your home. Your Ridgeback should also know how to walk politely on a leash without dragging you around the neighborhood.

Sit

Photo Courtesy of Jacki Hill

The first command that most owners teach their dog is sit. This is because it's one of the more simple commands and most dogs learn how to perform the correct behavior rather quickly. If you plan on competing in obedience, your dog will be required to know this command, but it's also helpful around the house when you may want to ask your dog to sit and wait patiently while you attach his leash or serve his dinner. Asking your dog to sit while you open the door can help teach him not to bolt. It's also a helpful skill if you want to take your dog to a local café or relax in the park. The sit also positions the dog in a way that makes it easier for him to make eye contact with you, so he can focus on what you want him to do next.

There are two popular ways to teach your Ridgeback how to sit. You may want to use only positive reinforcement, or you may want to combine that with negative reinforcement. Just be careful of your timing if you choose to use negative reinforcement. The most popular method of teaching your dog to sit is to have her stand in front of you and hold a treat in front of her face. Move the treat above her head, just out of reach, but not so high that she wants to jump up after it. Most dogs will sit in order to look up toward the treat. As your dog sits down, give her the verbal command, "Sit!"

There are two ways of introducing negative reinforcement to the first method. The first is to use your hand to place gentle pressure on your dog's hind end as you hold the treat up and give him the verbal command. Do not physically push his hind end to the ground, just apply gentle but firm pressure. Be sure to release the pressure the moment he begins to sit down. You can also try attaching your dog's leash and applying gentle upward pressure to his collar as you hold the treat up and give the verbal command. Most dogs will sit, both to look at the treat and get away from the pressure. Do not pull hard on the leash, just apply gentle pressure and release immediately when he performs the correct behavior.

Stay

The stay command is essential to teaching your dog self-control and patience. It can be helpful if you need your dog stay out your way, while doing housework for example, or if you're bringing in groceries and don't want her bolting out the open door. It's also helpful if you plan on taking her with you to cafes or coffee shops, or while you prepare her meals or welcome guests. You can test her self-control by putting her in a stay and tossing treats onto the floor or tossing his ball across the room. As she progresses in her training, you can also test her skills outside your home.

Many trainers choose to teach their dogs two versions of the 'stay' command. One is intended to teach the dog to stay in one place until he's released by the handler who is nearby. For example, if you want your dog to stay on his bed while you vacuum the house, you can place him in a stay and release him when you come back to his bed. The other version is usually intended for shorter periods of time and the dog can be released from any distance such as if you ask your dog to 'wait' before eating his food, or before calling him to you from a distance. The difference between these two commands is especially important if you plan on competing in any sports.

Stay is a command that builds on other basic commands. You can ask a dog to stay in a sitting, standing, or lying position. To teach the stay, simply ask her to sit, lie down, or stand and then give the command 'stay.' Many trainers use a flat open hand facing the dog to signal the command. At first, you only want your dog to stay for a second or two. Reward her if she does as you ask. If not, simply place her back into position and try again. With practice, you can increase the amount of time that you ask your dog to stay. You can also eventually move away and even try to leave the room. Remember to progress only as quickly as your dog can handle. Do not tempt her to move if she doesn't have a solid understanding of the command yet.

Lie Down

Generally, teaching your dog to lie down is the next step after teaching him to sit. This is because it's much easier to teach your dog this command once he already has an idea of what is expected of him in a sit. Teaching your dog to lie down is an important command, even if you don't plan on competing with him. You may need to ask your dog to lie down at the vet's office, or even in the car. You can also use this command as a first step in tricks such as crawl or roll over.

To teach your Ridgeback how to lie down, ask him to sit first. From the sitting position, hold a treat in front of his face and lower it down to the ground. You want to lure him into the down position as you give him the command 'lie down' or 'down.' Some dogs may try to stand up and then lower their head to the ground. If your dog tries to stand, simply put him back into a sitting position and try again. Some dogs may also try to crouch, rather than lie all the way down, so only reward him once his elbows touch the ground.

Come

Photo Courtesy of Channing Mae Malz

The 'come' command, or recall, is without a doubt the most important command you can teach your dog. Your dog must always come when you call, no matter what. A solid recall may even save your dog's life in certain situations. Some Ridgebacks have high-prey drives, so you must be firm and consistent in your training to discourage them from ignoring you in favor of chasing a squirrel or rabbit. This command is easiest to teach with two people, so if you have a friend or family member that can help, your dog will have an easier time learning. It's also helpful to teach this command in an enclosed or fenced-off area, or to use a long leash, such as a tracking lead.

To teach your dog the recall, have your helper hold your dog some distance away from you. Call your dog's name and give the command 'come' as you excitedly pat your legs. The more enthusiastic you can be, the better. Have your helper hold on to your dog for just a moment before releasing her. The momentary restraint will increase your dog's excitement and will encourage her to run to you, rather than in another direction. As your dog runs toward you, continue calling her while backing away a few steps. Backing up a bit will force her to chase you, if only for a few steps. This will help excite her and encourage her to come to you. Once she reaches you, praise her and give her plenty of treats and attention. Now that your dog is with you, you can try restraining her while your helper calls her. This can be done back and forth until your dog understands what you're asking of her. As you progress, you can increase the distance between you and your helper and also increase the level of distractions.

Off/Down

Asking your Rhodesian Ridgeback to get off the furniture when told to do so is not only important as far as manners, but will help you maintain your position as pack leader. Pack leaders do not allow others to sleep or sit in their favorite spots, so you must ask your dog to move if he's in your way. Be sure to use a different command for asking your dog to get off the furniture than you use to ask him to lie down. For example, if you use 'down' to ask him to lie down, you may want to use 'off' to tell him to get off the sofa.

There are several different ways you can teach your dog to move out of your way. The first is to use positive reinforcement and lure him off the sofa using a treat. As he hops off, give him the verbal command and praise him when all four feet touch the floor. You can also use negative reinforcement to help him understand what you're asking. You can use a leash to apply gentle pressure toward the edge of the sofa as you give the command. Once again, when his feet hit the ground, you can reward him. Be sure to use a leash, rather than grab his collar with your hand. More resistant dogs may try to bite you. You can try pushing him gently toward the sofa with your hands but be aware that dominant dogs may try to snap at you for this too.

Give/Drop

Not only does the 'give' or 'drop' command help you maintain your position as pack leader, but it's also helpful if your Rhodesian Ridgeback has a habit of stealing things or picking them up on your walks. Certain sports, such as obedience and dock diving, will require your dog to be able to drop things on command. Furthermore, teaching your dog to drop things on command will also help prevent resource-guarding issues.

If your dog has something in his mouth that you'd like him to give up, do not try to grab it out of his mouth. He is likely to bite down harder onto the item and not let go, and he may also snap at you. Instead, you should offer a trade. Offer him a treat or a different type of item such as a chew treat or toy. Whatever you're offering must be higher in value to your dog than what he has, so don't try to offer him a rubber toy in exchange for the chicken leg he stole from the trash. Give your verbal command as you offer him the treat and reward him as soon as he drops whatever it was that he had in his mouth before. If he exhibits resource guarding behaviors, you may need to lure him a short distance away with the treat before you can take possession of the item. With repetition, your dog should eventually learn to drop whatever he has when you ask, simply because you might have something better to offer him.

Walk

Photo Courtesy of
Caroline Higgins

Walking politely on the leash is one of the most important skills to teach your Rhodesian Ridgeback. Ridgebacks are large, powerful dogs that can easily pull someone off their feet, so walking nicely on a loose leash is necessary. Dogs who pull on the leash or try to drag their handlers are also more likely to become excitable or aggressive when they encounter strange dogs or people on their walks. Dogs are also more likely to injure themselves by pulling hard on collars or harnesses that are not designed to be pulled on.

Patience is key when teaching your dog to walk nicely on the leash. You may only be able to get a step or two of loose-leash walking at a time, so relax and take your time. Begin walking with your dog and the moment she puts tension on the leash, simply stop. Do not move an inch. Your dog will probably get to the end of her leash and turn around and look at you in confusion. You can either call her back or wait until she comes back to you on her own. Once the leash is slack again, you can begin walking. Again, she'll probably try to pull, so you'll need to stop and wait for her to come back. You may not get very far during your first few training sessions, but eventually you'll need to stop less frequently.

If your dog is excitable or energetic, you may want to hold a quick play session before working on your leash manners to wear her out. A calmer dog will learn to walk politely more quickly than an excited one.

Advanced Commands

As your Ridgeback advances in his training, you may need to introduce more advanced commands to keep him interested and challenged. There is no limit to what you can teach your dog, so don't be afraid to get creative. You can try leaving the room during long stays or walking off-leash in safe areas. If you plan on competing with your dog, you can work on sport-specific commands. You can also try teaching your dog interesting tricks, such as shake or roll over. Rhodesian Ridgebacks are generally willing to learn anything, as long as they get to spend time with their family, so don't be afraid to make things interesting.

TER 12

Unwanted Behaviors

What Is Bad Behavior in Dogs?

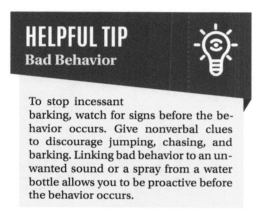

HELPFUL TIP
Bad Behavior

To stop incessant barking, watch for signs before the behavior occurs. Give nonverbal clues to discourage jumping, chasing, and barking. Linking bad behavior to an unwanted sound or a spray from a water bottle allows you to be proactive before the behavior occurs.

In dogs, bad behavior consists of actions that are considered unwanted, harmful, disrespectful, or dangerous. Some habits may be more of a minor annoyance, like excessive barking, but they can seriously impact your relationship with your family and your Rhodesian Ridgeback. More dangerous habits, such as running away or aggression, can actually put your Ridgeback's life at risk. All bad behaviors are at risk of escalating into more serious problems if they aren't corrected as soon as possible.

Bad habits don't develop overnight. They usually begin as something seemingly harmless that goes uncorrected. It takes time and a lack of consistent correction for bad behaviors to develop. The sooner these problems are dealt with, the less likely they are to escalate into more serious issues. Sandra Fikes of Kalahari Rhodesian Ridgebacks advises, "You must attend these problems as pups, socialize and go to a training class. Most of the problems I've encountered are a direct result of the owner not being aware or not doing their part in training." However, it should be noted that corrections are only valuable if they are consistent. If you only sporadically correct your dog for digging in the yard, he's probably going to be confused instead of understanding that his actions are wrong. Your dog may wonder why he's allowed to dig sometimes, but at other times gets punished. With a little patience, as well as firm and consistent corrections, most bad behaviors can be corrected before they become dangerous or life-threatening.

*Photo Courtesy of
Siobhan Swannell*

Finding the Root of the Problem

The only way to truly solve behavioral problems is to determine the cause of the behavior. Finding the root of the problems will help you develop a training plan to overcome the unwanted behavior. If you don't know what is causing your dog to act inappropriately, you'll never be able to completely eliminate his bad habits. For example, if you know your dog is likely to become aggressive when another dog tries to take his favorite toy, then you know where to focus your energy. However, if you honestly don't know why your dog keeps getting into fights, you're unlikely to be able to fix the problem. You may be able to temporarily solve the problem, but you won't have a long-term solution.

One potential cause for your Rhodesian Ridgeback's behavioral issues is your own behavior. As noted earlier, you may need to reflect on your own actions and reactions to determine whether you may be inadvertently sending the wrong signals to your dog. Reflecting on your own actions and behavior and being honest about how you may be affecting your dog is an important step in figuring out the cause of your dog's problems.

It's also possible that your dog's behavioral issues are caused by poor management of his environment. Controlling and changing your dog's behavior simply cannot be done if you don't control her environment. For instance, if you know that your dog becomes aggressive toward your other pets at feeding time, you may need to separate them until you are better able to control her behavior. Do not set your dog up for failure. You must always give your dog the chance to succeed and carefully controlling her environment will help her learn how to handle these situations correctly. Managing her environment is a lifelong commitment, especially when it comes to aggression. You must be committed to this duty and stay vigilant in order to prevent your dog from making a mistake.

Bad Behavior Prevention

Rather than correcting bad behavior, you should work to prevent it from developing in the first place. The time and effort involved in preventing bad habits is far less than what it would take to correct a bad habit once it has been established. Careful supervision and management of your dog's environment is essential to preventing bad behaviors. If you know your dog likes to dig in the trash, do not give him the opportunity to do so. Keep the trash somewhere he has no access to it. If you know what triggers your dog's bad behavior, you must avoid it until your dog is further along in his

Photo Courtesy of
Channing Mae Malz

training. If you are unsure of whether you can trust your dog in a given situation, it may be best to err on the side of caution and approach the situation at a later date when you are more certain of how your dog is going to act.

Consistency is also essential to preventing bad habits from developing. Without consistency, your dog cannot learn what is and is not appropriate behavior. If you allow your dog to jump on you when you get home from work, you can hardly be surprised when he jumps on your elderly neighbor in greeting. Training your dog is a time-consuming commitment and you must be willing to decide on the rules of the household and enforce them consistently. If you are only willing to put in the effort of correcting your dog's behavior when you feel like it, you're never going to see any significant change in his unwanted behaviors. Dog training is not a part-time gig. You may not have the motivation to work with your dog every single day, but your dog will likely have plenty of motivation to entertain himself if you don't. If you are consistent in your expectations and your training, you can expect consistency from your dog's behavior.

How to Properly Correct Your Rhodesian Ridgeback

When correcting your Rhodesian Ridgeback's bad behavior, it's important to keep the severity of your corrections in line with the severity of her actions. Different actions will require different corrections, but you need to use your best judgment to determine how serious your correction needs to be. Under no circumstances should you ever hit or kick your dog. Even if your dog is displaying dangerous or aggressive behavior, it's not appropriate to physically harm your dog. Your dog is unlikely to understand that you are correcting her, and she may react out of fear or aggression and bite you. Even the most extreme behavioral problems can be improved with a gentle touch and positive reinforcement.

When correcting your Ridgeback's bad behavior, you must be conscious of your timing. If you do not catch your dog in the act, you cannot correct him. If you come home and see your dog has destroyed the sofa, you must simply clean up the mess and move on. Dogs do not have a good understanding of the past and present. Your dog will not understand that he's in trouble for destroying the furniture, he will just think you came home and started punishing him for no reason. However, if you come home and catch your dog with a throw pillow in his mouth, then you can feel free to correct him as needed.

As discussed previously, hitting, kicking, or yelling at your dog are not appropriate corrections. Proper corrections include loud noises, such as stomps, claps, or telling her 'no'. For more serious behaviors, many trainers recommend filling a spray bottle with water and spritzing your dog in the face when she acts out. It's a harsher correction than a loud noise or firm 'no' but won't hurt your dog in any way. It's just an unpleasant sensation that will help discourage your dog from repeating that behavior in the future. The only situation that calls for extreme corrections is fighting. If your dog gets into a fight, it may be appropriate to yell or spray your dog with a hose. Loud and sudden noises are often enough to startle the dogs out of the fight. Depending on the size of the other dog, serious injury or even death is a possibility, so use an appropriate level of correction to stop the fight.

Photo Courtesy of
Joanne Baker

Fixing Bad Habits

Patience and dedication are key to fixing your Rhodesian Ridgeback's bad habits. Bad behavior doesn't develop suddenly, nor will it be fixed suddenly. Regardless of whether you are training your dog yourself or with the help of a professional, you need to understand that it will take time to solve your dog's behavioral problems. It's important not to lose your motivation. The first few days or weeks can be frustrating, but be patient and you should soon see improvement, even if it is small.

It can be difficult to balance dog ownership with your professional and personal lives, but you must remember that your dog and his behavior are your responsibilities. Inconsistency in your dog's training is likely what allowed the bad habits to develop in the first place, so you must be willing to make up for that now. Even after your dog's behavior has improved, you will need to remain consistent in your training and dedicated to managing your dog's environment in order to prevent the bad habit from coming back and to prevent your dog from developing new unwanted behaviors.

When to Call a Professional

Any time you are struggling with your dog's training or behavior, you should be willing to call a trainer. Even if the behavior is simply annoying and is not putting anyone at risk, if you are having trouble getting it under control you should seek help. Trainers deal with bad habits of every type and will be able to help you find the root of the problem and develop a training plan to overcome it. The sooner you are willing to accept outside help, the sooner you can fix the problem and prevent it from escalating into something worse.

If your dog's fearful, destructive, or aggressive behavior is affecting the happiness or safety of your family, you need to seek help immediately. Even seemingly harmless behavior, such as growling, can escalate quickly, so the sooner you call for help the better. Dangerous behavior can be difficult for the average dog owner to manage, so it's best to seek out someone who has experience in managing and correcting these types of habits. Even fearful behavior can become aggressive if the dog feels threatened or feels like she needs to defend herself. Regardless of the severity of his behavior, you need to seek help before someone gets hurt.

CHAPTER 12   Unwanted Behaviors

Rhodesian Ridgeback–Specific Bad Habits

Due to the Rhodesian Ridgeback's history as a hunting breed, some dogs can have a relatively high prey drive, which can make training difficult. It can be hard to keep your dog's attention when he's more focused on that squirrel on the other side of the park. According to Carol Vesely of Northstar Rhodesian Ridgebacks, "Their high prey drive can be a challenge. I don't feel they are the type of dog that you can have off-leash anywhere you go. My advice is to never have your Ridgeback off-leash for a minute unless you are in a secure, safe area that is either fenced in or there is nothing around where the dog can hurt themselves." Some dogs may have higher prey drives than others, so it's important to consider your individual's dog's interest in prey when deciding whether or not to let him off-leash. If your Ridgeback does have a high prey drive, you can also embrace it and compete with him in sports such as lure coursing, where he can chase his "prey" to his heart's content.

It's not uncommon for Rhodesian Ridgebacks to use their hunting instincts to get into trouble. The breed's strong sense of smell often leads Ridgebacks to getting into trash cans. Combine this superior sense of smell with the breed's love of food and you have a recipe for disaster. Be sure to keep your household's trash out of your dog's reach. Keeping the trash can in a cabinet may work, but some dogs even figure out how to open cabinet doors. There are trashcans on the market that lock, or are designed to be difficult for dogs to get into, so you may need to do some research to see what will work for your dog. The trash can be a tempting source of snacks, but your dog may also be able to swallow something dangerous like cooked bones, chemicals, or toxic foods.

Rhodesian Ridgebacks can also be quite destructive if left to their own devices. Many Ridgeback owners have come home to find dog beds, chew toys, or even throw pillows torn to shreds. If your dog becomes destructive, it's possible that she's simply bored. You may need to increase the amount of physical and mental exercise she gets in order to allow her to rest peacefully while you're away. You may also want to consider restricting her access to your house until she can be trusted to be left alone. Limiting your Ridgeback's access to just one room, or even keeping her crated, while you're away from home will help keep her destructive tendencies under control. Some dogs become especially destructive during teething, so be sure to provide your puppy with plenty of appropriate chewing options to prevent her from picking up and destroying household or personal items.

CHAPTER 13
Traveling with Rhodesian Ridgebacks

Dog Carriers and Car Restraints

When traveling with your Rhodesian Ridgeback in the car, you have a few different options for how you can restrain him. It's important to note that certain types of kennels or barriers will fit differently in different types of vehicles, so you may need to do some research to make sure that the one you choose fits securely in your car. Some dogs prefer seclusion during their travels, while others like to look out the window, so remember to take your individual dog's preferences into consideration. You may also be able to start with one type of restraint and move to another as your Ridgeback becomes a more confident and comfortable traveler.

One of the most popular methods of restraint may be one you recognize from your own home. The use of kennels or crates in cars is a common way to keep dogs safe until you reach your destination. Owners typically have the option of wire, plastic, or soft-sided crates. Some are designed specifically for use in the car, so they may be shaped differently or have ways to secure the crate to the vehicle. There are even companies that make heavy-duty metal crates designed to withstand the impact of a crash, but these can be quite costly. Some crates are designed to be placed in the cargo area of your vehicle, while others fit nicely in the back seat. The type of crate you choose will depend on the type of car you drive, as well as what works best for you and your dog. Dogs who like a bit of seclusion may prefer a more enclosed plastic or metal crate, or even just a blanket tossed over their wire crate. Dogs who like to see what's going on around them may prefer the openness of a wire kennel. No matter what size crate you choose, make sure it's big enough for your Ridgeback to be able to comfortably stand up and turn around. Feel free to place his favorite blanket or even a towel in his crate to make him more comfortable. Towels can also help with cleanup should your dog become carsick. Making the trip as comfortable as possible is an important part of teaching your dog to enjoy his time in the car.

If you would prefer that your Rhodesian Ridgeback have a little more freedom, or your vehicle isn't big enough for a crate, consider using a barrier. Barriers allow your dog more room than a typical kennel, but still prevent her from jumping into your lap while you're driving or getting into your groceries. Most barriers are made of metal, either bars or mesh, and are easy to install. Many barriers are pressure-mounted, which means they won't damage or alter your vehicle. Barriers can be installed to keep your dog confined to either the cargo area or the back seat, depending on the

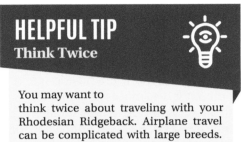

HELPFUL TIP
Think Twice

You may want to think twice about traveling with your Rhodesian Ridgeback. Airplane travel can be complicated with large breeds. Always check with the airline well before your scheduled flight. If traveling by car, allow plenty of exercise before and during the trip to keep your dog content.

type you buy. There are a few downsides to using a barrier. Dogs who get carsick or like to chew may make a mess of your car seats. It's advisable to invest in waterproof seat covers if you're going to use this restraint method. Another potential downside is that you need to be careful opening your car doors. If your dog tries to bolt out of the car as soon as you open the door, she may be able to push past you before you can get a leash on her.

The third type of restraint you might consider is using a doggy seat belt. Doggy seat belts resemble a short leash with a seat belt latchplate on one end that can be clipped into the seat belt buckle like a regular seat belt would. The other end is exactly like a leash and attaches to your dog's harness. If you choose to use a seat belt, be sure to always attach it to a harness, rather than a collar. If you get into an accident or have to do quick maneuvering to avoid one, your dog may be thrown forward or sideways and the pressure from the seat belt can serious injure his neck. Harnesses distribute that pressure over more surface area, so they're safer for your dog. One benefit of using seat belts is that if your dog likes to bolt out the car door as soon as you reach your destination, the seat belt allows you to open the car door and attach his leash before releasing him.

Whichever method of restraint you choose, just remember to use it consistently. Keeping your dog contained while in the car is essential for keeping you, him, and other drivers safe. If your Rhodesian Ridgeback is loose in the car, he may try to jump into your lap or out the window. If you get into an accident, he may also be able to escape from your vehicle and run off into traffic. Most Ridgebacks love traveling, but you must prioritize your pet's safety as you would any other family member's.

Preparing Your Rhodesian Ridgeback for Car Rides

Traveling with your Rhodesian Ridgeback should be as stress-free for everyone as possible. To minimize stress, be sure to thoroughly prepare your dog. The more you practice good car manners, socialization, and basic commands, the more likely you are to enjoy your time with your dog. Try to introduce your dog to new situations slowly and at a young age, if possible. Sandra Fikes of Kalahari Rhodesian Ridgebacks advises, "Early good experiences are the key." The more time and effort you put in to preparing your dog for travel, the more enjoyable it will be for everyone.

Before you take your Rhodesian Ridgeback for his first ride, you need to consider how much experience he has had with cars in the past. If he's a puppy or just an inexperienced traveler, you need to put a little extra time into preparing him for his first trip. Some dogs, once they become expe-

Photo Courtesy of
Kaitlyn Lamping

rienced travelers, are able to eat and drink on the go without a problem. Other may struggle with carsickness no matter how much experience they have. To prevent your dog from becoming carsick, it may be best to withhold or limit his food and water before your trip. As a precaution, you may want to bring a few towels to aid in cleanup should your dog get sick. To limit the mess in your car, you may want to invest in waterproof seat covers, or cover your seats or floors with blankets or towels. If you choose to travel with your dog in a crate, you will at least be able to limit the mess to the confines of the crate.

As with children, it's a good idea to give your Ridgeback the chance to go to the bathroom before you get in the car. This way, you won't need to make an emergency stop on the way to your destination. If you're going on a long-distance road trip, you'll still need to stop every few hours to give her a chance to relieve herself. If possible, stick to the same potty break schedule you keep at home.

Before you begin your road trip, you need to double-check all kennels, barriers, or seat belts and make sure everything is in working order. If you're traveling long distances, ensure you have all of the supplies you need for the duration of your trip including your dog's collar, leash, waste bags, bowls, and food. If your dog is able to drink while in the car without becoming sick, you may want to bring a bottle or bowl of water along.

It's also important to make sure your dog has been thoroughly prepared for a trip in the car. If you've never taken him in the car before, or he's never worn the harness his seat belt will attach to, you may be in for a frustrating and disruptive road trip. Get your dog used to jumping in and out of the car, or have him wait patiently in his kennel while your car is parked in the driveway. The more preparation you do with your dog, the more confident he will be when it's time to hit the road. In general, Rhodesian Ridgebacks make excellent travel companions, but you must do your homework before setting off. According to Carol Vesely of Northstar Rhodesian Ridgebacks, "What many people like about this breed is their athleticism yet their ability to be a couch potato. They are able to be quiet for long periods without driving the owner crazy." In the weeks or days before your trip, make sure you and your dog are thoroughly prepared for your adventures together.

Flying and Hotel Stays

Before you leave home, you need to be sure that the airline you're flying or the hotel you're staying at is dog friendly. If you do this well in advance, you'll be able to make the necessary changes ahead of time without the stress of last-minute changes to your travel plans. Most airlines and hotels charge extra fees for dogs, so be sure to ask about these and budget accordingly. You may need to pay in advance for your dog, or you may be able to pay when you arrive at the airport or hotel.

If you plan on flying with your Rhodesian Ridgeback, you should be aware that your dog will probably be traveling in the cargo hold of the plane. Modern planes have special climate-controlled sections of the cargo hold that are specifically designed to accommodate animals, so as long as your dog is healthy enough for travel, he will be fine. Only small animals, usually under 20 pounds, are permitted to travel in the cabin of the plane. The exception to this rule is service animals. As long as you let the airline know in advance that you plan on traveling with your dog, you should have no problems. However, be sure to get him used to his kennel before traveling. You don't want his first experience with a crate to be on the way to the airport.

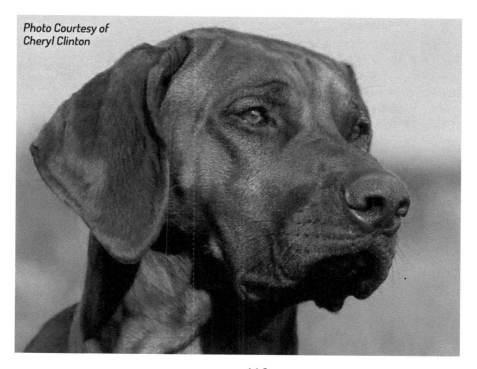

Photo Courtesy of Cheryl Clinton

Photo Courtesy of Stephanie Egger

Most airlines have strict guidelines on the size and shape of kennels, so be sure check with the airline you'll be using to see if your kennel will be allowed or if you need to make any changes. Depending on your destination, you may also need certain health documents signed by your veterinarian. Finding out this type of information at the last minute can be disastrous, so be sure to speak with an airline representative well in advance to make sure you have everything in order.

There are many hotels across the country at all price points that are considered dog-friendly. Some may charge minor fees for dogs, while others allow pets to stay free, but usually only in certain rooms. Some hotels even offer their furry guests complimentary treats. No matter how dog-friendly the hotel is, it's your responsibility to make sure your dog is a respectful guest. Bringing an out-of-control, untrained dog into a hotel will leave a negative impression on hotel staff, and you will be responsible for any damages caused by your dog during your stay. Proper socialization and training are essential for any traveling dog owner, so be sure to prepare for your trip accordingly.

Kenneling vs. Dog Sitters

Photo Courtesy of Caroline Higgins

Travel can be stressful enough without having to worry about leaving your Rhodesian Ridgeback behind. However, finding the perfect boarding facility or pet sitter can help relieve that stress and let you focus on your trip. Whether you choose a boarding facility or pet sitter, it's important not to just make a reservation with the first person you speak to. Do your homework and make sure the person or people taking care of your dog in your absence will do a good job. Before deciding on where you will leave your dog, you also need to consider your Ridgeback's personality and what type of environment she prefers. If she's outgoing and playful, she may enjoy a boarding facility that does play groups, or even a cage-free facility so she can be with her new friends around the clock. Ask your family or friends who they leave their dog with when traveling.

Depending on your budget and the type of area you live in, you may have quite a few boarding facilities to choose from. Basic boarding facilities will likely be your cheapest option. These types of kennels keep your dog in a simple cage or run and provide him with two or three bathroom breaks per day. Often, dogs from the same family are allowed to stay in the same cage if they're big enough. Most of the time, basic boarding facilities are not staffed overnight. However, luxury boarding kennels are becoming more popular in many areas. These offer a range of services that may include elevated beds, televisions, and either group or individual play sessions. Cage-free boarding is rising in popularity as well. In cage-free facilities, your dog will spend his day playing in a pack environment and his nights sleeping next to his new friends. For friendly, energetic dogs, this is a perfect way to keep fit and busy in your absence. However, more reserved dogs may feel overwhelmed, so if your dog is shy, you may want to find a facility that offers one-on-one attention rather than group playtime. The more services a facility offers, the more expensive it will be, so consider your budget when searching for the right kennel.

If your dog is shy or nervous around strangers, she might be more comfortable in a home environment with a professional pet sitter than at a kennel. These pet sitters can come to your house each day to walk your dog and spend time with her, take your dog into their home for the duration of your absence, or stay overnight at your own home. This is a great option for shy dogs, or those who are stressed out by change. If you have other pets, or household needs, such as watering plants or bringing in the mail, pet sitters are also very helpful. In general, pet sitters are usually more expensive than boarding kennels. Their rates may also vary according to how many pets you have and what other tasks you request them to do.

No matter who you choose to leave your Ridgeback with, make sure you do your research to make sure your dog is in good hands. Most reputable pet sitters and boarding facilities will happily answer any questions you have and let you tour their facility or home. Ask them if they require any specific vaccinations or have other requirements prior to dropping your dog off. If you are interested in bringing items from home, such as toys or blankets, ask them about whether this is allowed or encouraged. If you do bring items from home, be sure to write your name or your dog's name on everything so it can be returned to you at the end of your dog's stay. Some facilities allow you to choose to feed their food of choice or bring food from home, so be sure to ask about this and mention any allergies or sensitivities your dog may have. Many boarding facilities and pet sitters also offer trial days, where you just drop your dog off for a few hours to make sure it's a good fit for everyone.

Photo Courtesy of
Michelle Gasaway

CHAPTER 14
Nutrition

Importance of Good Diet

A healthy and balanced diet is essential to your Rhodesian Ridge-back's well-being. Your dog needs the correct balance of vitamins and minerals to build and maintain healthy bones and muscles and a shiny coat. Fats and proteins nourish your dog's body and give him the energy to keep up with you and your family or perform in the show ring.

Without a properly balanced diet, dogs are at risk of developing long-term and even life-threatening conditions. Though not always diet-related, pancreatitis, kidney or bladder stones, and heart disease can all occur due to an imbalance of nutrients in the diet. Dogs with immune system deficiencies may also develop food allergies or sensitivities. Although you cannot entirely prevent your dog from falling ill, feeding him a balanced diet will give him the best chance at leading a long and healthy life.

Many pet food manufacturers label their dog foods as suitable for "all life stages." Foods with this label may or may not be appropriate for your Rhodesian Ridgeback, depending on his age and quality of health. Do not expect to feed your dog the same food for his entire life. As dogs age and their health changes, their diets may need to be adjusted accordingly. Foods targeting dogs of certain age groups, such as puppies and seniors, typically contain a slightly different balance of nutrients and calories, so they may be more appropriate for your dog's needs. Many vets recommend switching a dog to senior food at around seven or eight years of age. Senior foods typically contain fewer calories and may include more fiber or joint support. For large dogs, such as Rhodesian Ridgebacks, most manufacturers recommend feeding puppy food until about one year of age, at which point they can be switched to adult food, or one labeled for all life stages.

Commercial pet foods have been developed by teams of nutritionists and scientists to meet a certain standard. The Association of American Feed Control Officials (AAFCO) sets the standard of all commercial pet foods sold in the United States. If a food does not meet the requirements set by AAFCO, it must be recalled. Since there are no laws regulating homemade diets, if you choose to feed your Rhodesian Ridgeback a home-cooked or raw diet, you must do your research to ensure that you are providing him with the correct balance of nutrients. If you ever have any doubts about the quality of the food you are providing your Ridgeback, don't be afraid to ask your veterinarian or a veterinary nutritionist for advice.

Different Types of Commercial Food

The most popular type of food for dogs, by an enormous margin, is kibble. When you think of dog food, you probably picture the small, round nuggets of crunchy food. The reason that kibble is so popular is its convenience. It's easy to come home after a long day at work and give your dog his usual scoops of kibble and then get to work on household chores. Some dog owners even choose to leave a bowl of food out so their dogs can eat whenever they want. However, Susan Landers of Pistol Packin' Puppies recommends against this. She says, "Don't free-feed. Ridgebacks are gluttons. They will eat as long as there is food. Feed the recommended amount even if they still seem hungry." Another reason kibble is so popular is the variety of options available. If your dog needs a certain protein or suffers from a heart condition, you can find a kibble designed to suit his needs. There are even

Photo Courtesy of
Kaitlyn Lamping

low-calorie kibbles for dogs who need to lose weight. Kibble is available in a wide variety of quality levels and price points, so consider your budget before committing to a certain type of food.

Canned food is another popular, convenient option. It's softer than kibble, so it's a good option for dogs with dental problems. It also tends to be a bit more palatable, so it often appeals to picky dogs. Like kibble, there is a nearly endless variety of canned foods designed for every dietary need. Canned food contains more moisture than kibble, so it's often a good choice for older dogs, or those who may not drink enough water during the day. It should be noted that canned food tends to stick to dogs' teeth more than kibble, so if you feed a strict diet of canned food, your dog may need more frequent dental cleanings.

Fresh, refrigerated diets are rising in popularity among owners who want to feed their dogs a homecooked meal, but simply don't have the time or desire to do so. You can find these types of food in the refrigerated section of your local pet store. Like canned food, fresh food is generally softer than kibble. It's typically packaged in tightly packed rolls, which can be sliced into appropriately sized portions. After cutting off your dog's meal, simply seal the roll and place it back into the refrigerator for next time. Fresh food is often more expensive than either kibble or canned food, so you may need to consider this when deciding what to feed your Ridgeback.

Commercial raw diets are also becoming more popular. Typically, these consist of a carefully formulated blend of meat, organs, bones, and vegetables. They do not generally contain any excess grains or carbohydrates. This nutritionally balanced mixture is then formed into either patties or nuggets and frozen. Many pet owners and veterinarians alike are seeing the benefits of feeding their dogs what their ancestors ate. Homemade raw diets can be expensive and time-consuming, so commercial raw food provides owners a way to feed their dog their desired diet without committing to hours of food preparation. Along with the raw food in your local pet store's freezer section, you may also find goat's milk to supplement your dog's diet, as well as raw bones for recreational chewing and to keep your pet's teeth clean and healthy. Commercial raw diets are made from a variety of different proteins to accommodate dogs with food sensitivities.

Homemade Foods and Recipes

When you make your dog's food at home, you know exactly what goes into it and whether or not it contains any ingredients that your dog is sensitive to. However, homemade diets are often more expensive than commercial diets and are much more labor intensive. You need to consider how much time, effort, and money you're willing to invest in your dog's diet before you commit to feeding a homemade diet. It's also crucial that a homemade diet contain the proper balance of nutrients. Diet imbalances typically do not show up right away, but they can have long-term or even permanent effects on your dog's health. If you have any doubts about whether your Ridgeback's homemade diet is nutritionally balanced, you may want to consult a veterinary nutritionist.

As noted earlier, a popular type of homemade dog food is the raw diet. Raw diets are typically categorized as either Prey Model Raw (PMR) or Biologically Appropriate Raw (BARF). PMR diets are intended to mirror a wild dog's diet of whole prey animals. The balance of meat, organs, and bones reflect the approximate percentages of each in an entire prey animal. The only major difference between BARF and PMR diets is the amount of fruits and vegetables that are fed. BARF allows for a certain percentage of a dog's diet to be plant-based, while the PMR diet does not. Raw diets are often supplemented with bone broth, raw goat's milk, or fish stock. Raw feeders also frequently provide large bones for recreational chewing and to help clean their dog's teeth.

The ingredients of cooked homemade diets are similar to raw diets as the food is primarily meat based, sometimes with veggies. The major difference is that cooked diets often allow for a significant percentage of the diet to be made up of carbohydrates such as potatoes, barley, or rice. Owners who feed cooked diets often supplement their dogs' meals with vitamin mixes, kelp or seaweed, or dairy products such as yogurt or kefir. As with a raw diet, you must do your research to ensure your dog's meals are balanced, or consult a professional.

People Food—Harmful and Acceptable Kinds

Whether or not feeding your Ridgeback people food is a good idea is a topic of hot debate. Some owners are comfortable feeding their dogs a variety of people food, while others refuse to do so at all. However, before you take your stand on the topic, it's important to understand there are types of people food that can be beneficial to your dog and also types that can be harmful.

Unless you're feeding your dog a strict PMR diet, you may be fine feeding your dog fruits and vegetables. Certain fruits and vegetables make great snacks and treats, especially for dogs needing to trim their waistlines. Vegetables such as broccoli, sweet potatoes, peas, and carrots are safe and delicious. Many dogs also find spinach, green beans, zucchini, and cucumber appealing. Fruit should be fed less frequently than vegetables because of the higher sugar content. However, safe fruits include apples, bananas, strawberries, watermelon, and blueberries. Pineapple, cantaloupe, raspberries, and blackberries can also make healthy treats or snacks. It should be noted that not all fruits and vegetables are safe for dogs to consume. Onions, garlic, and grapes can be toxic to dogs if consumed. Pitted fruits, like cherries or peaches, are safe, but only if the pit has been removed.

Some types of people food are okay for dogs to eat, but only in small amounts. Cheese and peanut butter are popular treats, but they can be quite high in calories, so they must only be fed in moderation. Foods with a particularly high fat content can negatively impact a dog's endocrine system. Salty foods, such as popcorn and bacon, should also be limited. Dairy should also be limited, since some dogs tolerate it well while it may cause digestive upset in others.

Most dog owners are aware that chocolate is toxic to dogs, but there are a number of people foods that should be kept away from your pets. Foods containing caffeine or the artificial sweetener xylitol are incredibly toxic to dogs. Coffee, tea, and sugar-free gum and candy should be kept away from your Ridgeback. Alcohol is also poisonous to dogs, so keep your liquor cabinet locked tightly. If you suspect your dog may have gotten into something toxic, contact your veterinarian or local emergency veterinary clinic as soon as possible. The sooner your dog can receive treatment, the more likely it is that he will survive.

Photo Courtesy of Mike Krzyza

Weight Management

According to the Association for Pet Obesity Prevention, approximately 54 percent of American dogs are considered obese, or more than 30 percent above their ideal weight. Obesity can cause a variety of related conditions and can severely limit your Ridgeback's ability to enjoy life. Excess weight is hard on joints and even young, overweight dogs may have difficulty getting up or moving around. However, obesity is completely preventable, as long as you can keep a close eye on your dog's weight and adjust her diet accordingly. It can be tempting to give in to that adorable, begging face, but you must resist. Rhodesian Ridgebacks love their food, so even if they act hungry, it's unlikely that they are starving. To determine if your dog is at the correct weight, view her from the top and sides. She should have a visible waist from above and a defined tuck from the side. The ribs should be easily felt. If you're unsure of whether your dog is at a healthy weight, ask your veterinarian.

In addition to a healthy diet, your dog should receive between 30 minutes and two hours of exercise every day. This can include playtime, training sessions, and walks or hikes. The more your dog moves, the more calories she burns, so the more she can eat. If you can't stand to see your dog eating such meager amounts, then you need to increase her exercise so that she can burn the extra calories you insist on feeding her.

Proper portion size is the single largest factor in managing your dog's weight. It's essential that you feed your dog only as much as he needs to maintain his weight. Most pet food manufacturers label pet food containers with suggested serving sizes. These should be used as a rough guideline to determine how much to feed your dog. Be aware that these suggested amounts do not take into consideration your dog's age, activity level, and health conditions or physical limitations. It's a good starting point, but if you notice your dog gaining or losing weight, you may need to adjust his portions accordingly. If you have any doubts about whether your Ridgeback is at a healthy weight, consult a veterinarian or nutritionist.

When calculating your Ridgeback's daily caloric intake, don't forget about his treats. Treats are often forgotten when figuring out your dog's meal portions, so be sure to count those extra calories. If your dog is on a strict diet, you can always use a portion of his daily amount of kibble to use during training sessions. You can also use healthy, low-calorie options such as fruit or vegetables.

CHAPTER 15
Grooming Your Rhodesian Ridgeback

Coat Basics

Rhodesian Ridgebacks are a shorthaired breed that require very little grooming. Their smooth coats, with their signature ridge along the spine, are easy to maintain with regular brushing and an occasional bath. Having a shorthaired dog means you won't be brushing tangles or mats, but you will still have to deal with shedding. According to Carol Vesely of Northstar Rhodesian Ridgebacks, "Ridgebacks do shed. Their hair is short and firm, not long and silky. It's not the kind of hair you can brush off your sweater. The tiny hairs stick into wool and need to be pulled out. Black wool clothing and Ridgebacks don't go together very well!" Rhodesian Ridgebacks are considered to be average shedders, so while you won't find yourself covered from head to toe in dog hair, you'll still find evidence of your Ridgeback around the house and on furniture. You may find that your Ridgeback sheds more during certain times of the year, typically in the spring and fall, and might need to brush or bathe your dog more frequently at those times.

Photo Courtesy of
Steve Warwick

Photo Courtesy of
Linda Larras

Bathing and Brushing

Even though Rhodesian Ridgebacks have short hair, you will still need to fit regular brushing sessions into your weekly schedule. Ridgebacks' short, tight coats typically only need to be brushed once or twice per week to stay healthy. Brushing such a shorthaired dog may seem like a waste of time, but it stimulates blood flow to the skin and evenly distributes the coat's natural oils. It also removes dead hair and dander, which would otherwise be shed around the house.

One of the best tools to use for grooming a Rhodesian Ridgeback is a rubber curry brush. Rubber brushes are available in a wide variety of shapes and sizes, so you should be able to find one that fits comfortably in your hand. This type of brush can be used on a dry coat, as well as during a bath. To use, grip the brush firmly and move it in circular motions around your dog's coat. Use gentle pressure and be sure to avoid bony or sensitive areas, such as the lower legs and head. In the bath, this brush can be used to distribute shampoo throughout the coat and remove dead hair and skin. You may also be interested in using grooming gloves to brush your Ridgeback. Grooming gloves are fabric gloves with textured rubber palms and fingers. They work the same as rubber curry brushes and are great for baths because they won't slip out of your hands. Both brushes provide a soothing massage sensation for your dog, so don't be surprised when he starts getting excited about grooming sessions! Shedding blades can also be used on a Ridgeback, but care must be taken not to scratch or irritate the skin. Use gentle pressure with a shedding blade and avoid sensitive parts of the body such as the head, belly, legs, and tail.

HELPFUL TIP
Low-maintenance Shedder

Although your Rhodesian Ridgeback will not require professional grooming, it will need thorough weekly brushing with a rubber curry comb to keep the shedding to a minimum. Wipe your dog down weekly with a damp cloth to maintain a lustrous coat. Your Ridgeback will need professional attention every four to eight weeks for nail trims, ear cleanings, and anal gland checks.

Rhodesian Ridgebacks require only the occasional bath to keep them looking and smelling clean. Depending on how dirty your Ridgeback likes to get when she plays, you will likely only need to bathe her every four to eight weeks. Most professional groomers do not recommend bathing your dog any more frequently than every four weeks because bathing your dog too often can strip the coat of its natural oils and can result in dry, itchy skin. Going any longer than eight weeks between baths is also not recommended. Regular bathing not only helps clean the coat of excess oils, dirt, and dander, but it also gives you a chance to go over your dog from head to toe. You'll be able to spot any potential skin or coat issues in their early stages. You may need to bathe your Ridgeback more or less frequently depending on the season and the weather. With each brushing session, you'll be able to assess her coat to determine whether she's due for a bath.

When bathing your Rhodesian Ridgeback, it's important that you get the shampoo down to the skin, rather than just on the surface of the coat. This is where tools such as the rubber curry brush can come in handy. Brushes or grooming gloves will help massage the shampoo through the coat to the skin. When shampooing your dog, be sure to avoid getting water or shampoo in his eyes or ears. Shampoo can sting and potentially damage your dog's eye and excess moisture in the ears can lead to ear infections. Some groomers place cotton balls in the dog's ears before bathing to help keep water out. If you choose to do this, be sure to remove the cotton balls after the bath. After shampooing, you'll need to rinse your dog thoroughly as any shampoo left in the coat may cause irritation. A good rule of thumb is to rinse until you think your dog is free of shampoo, and then rinse once more to be sure. The use of conditioner is optional, but if your Ridgeback's coat seems dry or damaged, or he's suffering from itchy skin, conditioner can be quite beneficial. Once again, be sure to rinse all the conditioner from his coat. Since Ridgebacks have such a short coat, towel drying is usually sufficient.

The type of shampoo and conditioner you use will depend on your own preferences, as well as the health of your dog's skin. There are many different types of shampoos available, so if you need one for itchy skin, odor control, or even skunk odor removal, you'll be able to find what you're looking for. It's important to check the ingredients of the shampoo before buying, especially If your Ridgeback has sensitive skin. You want a shampoo with more natural ingredients and fewer chemicals to reduce the chances of skin irritation or allergic reaction. It should be noted that many natural shampoos do not use the chemicals necessary to make bubbles, so even though they may not be as sudsy as other shampoos, they're still cleaning effectively. You may also want to invest in a waterless shampoo for use between baths. Waterless shampoo is usually packaged in a spray bottle and can simply be spritzed onto your dog and wiped off.

Trimming the Nails

There are two methods of trimming your Rhodesian Ridgeback's nails. Both methods have positive and negative aspects, so you may want to try them both before deciding which you prefer. The most common method is to use scissor-type nail clippers. These cut well and typically do not carry the risk of crushing or damaging the nail. (Avoid guillotine-style nail clippers for this reason.) They are easy to use, even for owners inexperienced with trimming their dogs' nails. One downside of scissor-type clippers is that it is easy to cut the nail too short, clipping the nail's blood supply, or quick. This

can be painful for the dog and she may become resistant to nail trimming if she is cut to the quick frequently.

The other method of nail trimming is to use a grinder, such as a Dremel. With a grinder, you are able to take only a small layer off the nail each time, reducing the chances of cutting the nail too short. You are also able to round the edges of the nail as you go, so your dog won't scratch your floors, furniture, or family. Sandra Fikes of Kalahari Rhodesian Ridgebacks says, "I like to use a Dremel with a diamond drum as Rhodesian Ridgebacks' nails can be hard." Care must be taken not to grind or scratch a dog's skin. The speed of the spinning head can scrape the skin very quickly if you aren't careful.

There are a few different factors to consider when deciding how often to trim your Rhodesian Ridgeback's nails. Some owners choose to trim nails weekly, while others do it every two or three weeks. If your daily walks include a lot of time on pavement, you may not need to trim your dog's nails as frequently as you would if you're walking on grass or dirt. This is because the abrasive surface of the pavement may file down your dog's nails as he walks. Different dogs also grow nails at different paces, so if you have multiple dogs in your household, you may need to adjust your nail trimming schedule to each dog's specific needs. Most groomers recommend trimming nails at least every 4-6 weeks. Any longer between trims and the nails may become long enough to cause discomfort.

To trim your Ridgeback's nails, you need to first examine the nail to determine how far into the nail the blood supply, or quick, reaches. Most Ridgebacks have dark or black nails, so it may be difficult to see the quick. Regardless of what tool you're using to trim your dog's nails, hold his paw gently but firmly. As you clip or grind each nail, be sure to take just a thin layer off each time to avoid cutting the quick. With each layer, keep an eye out for a dark spot in the center of the nail. Once you see the dark spot, you've nearly reached the quick so you can quit and move on to the next nail. Be sure to use plenty of praise and offer treats to reward your dog for her patience.

If you have any questions about trimming your Rhodesian Ridgeback's nails or would rather have a professional take care of the job, consult your veterinarian or groomer. Nail trims are typically quite inexpensive, and many clinics and grooming shops even accept walk-ins for this service. Most places will offer you the choice of using either a clipper or a grinder, though more grooming salons are switching to grinders. Veterinary staff and groomers are both professionals in dog handling, so if you're struggling to control your dog while you trim her nails, it may be best to have a professional teach her how to stand patiently.

Brushing Their Teeth

Good dental hygiene is essential to your Rhodesian Ridgeback's health and overall well-being. Over 80 percent of dogs over the age of three suffer from some form of dental disease. Thankfully, dental problems can easily be prevented with regular dental care, including yearly veterinary exams and daily brushing. Teeth brushing must be done every day in order to have any real effect on the plaque and tartar on your dog's teeth. Without daily brushing, plaque and tartar can build up on your dog's teeth. The bacteria present in tartar will lead to inflammation of the gums, also known as periodontal disease, and can even enter the bloodstream to infect other parts of the body. Dogs with periodontal disease may also experience difficulty eating due to pain or loose teeth. However, regular at-home dental care and visits to a veterinarian can help prevent periodontal disease and its associated health problems.

There are many different types of toothbrush and toothpastes available on the market, so you may need to do some research before deciding which one is best for you and your dog. Doggy toothpaste comes in a variety of flavors, such as vanilla, chicken, and peanut butter. Choose an appetizing flavor to help entice your dog and encourage him to enjoy having his teeth brushed. You should never use human toothpaste on your dog, as it contains ingredients that can be harmful to dogs. A paste made from baking soda and water also works well in a pinch. You also have quite a few different choices for toothbrushes. You can find toothbrushes similar in appearance to those used by humans, or you can find rubber or silicone brushes that can be put over the tip of your finger. Consider the size of your dog's mouth and whether or not you want to stick your finger in her mouth when making your decision.

Before brushing your Ridgeback's teeth for the first time, let her sniff and lick the toothpaste off the toothbrush. If she likes the flavor, she'll be more accepting of the toothbrush in her mouth. Once she's comfortable licking the brush, you can try brushing a tooth or two. Start slow and only progress as much as she will allow. Use plenty of praise and positive reinforcement. With practice, you'll be able to brush all of her teeth and she may even look forward to the process.

No matter what your at-home dental routine is like, your dog will still need regular professional dental cleanings done by your veterinarian. If you choose not to brush your dog's teeth, your vet will probably recommend that you bring your dog in every 6-12 months to have his teeth cleaned. Daily brushing may enable your dog to go longer between professional cleanings, but it's still a good idea to have one or two exams per year to make sure your dog's teeth and mouth are healthy.

Cleaning Ears and Eyes

Some Rhodesian Ridgebacks can be prone to ear infections, especially if they enjoy swimming or are bathed frequently. If moisture enters the ear canal, it can create the ideal environment for yeast and bacteria to grow. Ear infections can be painful and can even cause permanent damage if neglected for too long, so it's best to prevent them if possible. It's a good idea to clean your dog's ears after any water-related activity, just to remove any excess moisture. While cleaning your dog's ears, if you notice any odor, redness, or swelling, or he seems to be scratching his ears a lot, he may already have an ear infection. Ear infections are relatively easy to treat. A veterinarian will be able to determine whether the infection is due to yeast or bacteria, and can prescribe the appropriate medication.

Your local pet store or favorite online retailer likely has a few different ear cleaners to choose from. It's important to choose a cleaner that does not contain alcohol, as it can burn sensitive ears. If you're having trouble choosing an ear cleaner, ask your vet or groomer for advice. They'll recommend a quality ear cleaner and will also be able to show you how to clean your dog's ears.

To clean your Ridgeback's ears, wet a cotton ball in the ear cleaning solution and squeeze out the excess. Wipe around the ear canal, as well as

Photo Courtesy of Adam Sexton

inside as far as you can reach. Don't worry about hurting your dog. As long as you are gentle, you won't hurt him or be able to reach any of the delicate structures of the ear with your finger. You can, however, damage the eardrum or other structures of the ear if you use a cotton swab, so it's crucial that you only use a cotton ball. After wiping out your dog's ear, go over everything with a dry cotton ball to ensure that you have removed as much moisture as possible. Your dog may shake or rub his ears on the carpet or furniture afterwards, so wiping up as much of the cleaner as you can will help prevent it from being distributed throughout your house.

Most Rhodesian Ridgebacks do not need to have their eyes cleaned. However, some may have runny eyes due to allergies or other health concerns. If your Ridgeback has watery eyes, you may need to clean her face regularly in order to prevent yeast from growing. If your dog develops reddish tear stains with a distinctive odor, she may have a small yeast infection. Although tear stains are not harmful to your dog, they are unpleasant, especially if they begin to smell. There are many different products on the market that you can use to wipe your dog's face. It's best not to use shampoo to clean the area, as you risk getting shampoo in your dog's eyes. A medicated wipe, or even just a damp cloth, will remove any dirt or grime and help prevent yeast.

When Professional Help Is Necessary

Although Rhodesian Ridgebacks are not difficult dogs to groom, they are quite large and can be rambunctious. There's no shame in asking for professional help if you can't or don't want to groom your Ridgeback yourself. In fact, taking your dog to a groomer is an excellent way to socialize him and teach him to respect others and tolerate being handled by people other than you. Groomers are also experts in teaching dogs how to stand patiently while being pampered. They are also knowledgeable in skin and coat care and can spot any potential problems or answer any questions you may have.

Groomers are also experts in handling difficult dogs. If you are struggling to get your dog to stand nicely while having her nails trimmed or while being brushed, you may want to consult a professional. Many groomers actually welcome difficult dogs because they understand how to calm them and teach them not to be afraid. Even if your dog is nervous the first few times she visits the groomer, after she develops a relationship with her groomer, she will probably look forward to her regular visits with her new friend.

CHAPTER 16
Basic Health Care

Visiting the Vet

Although many people only take their dogs to the vet when they are ill or injured, routine veterinary check-ups are essential to your Rhodesian Ridgeback's health. Depending on your dog's age and health, most veterinarians recommend an exam every 6-12 months. It may seem frivolous to take your dog the vet that often if he's not showing any signs of health con-

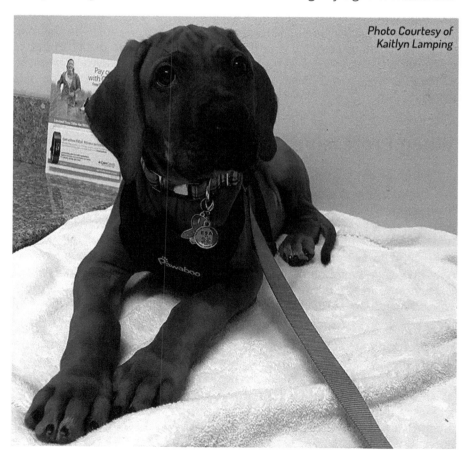

Photo Courtesy of Kaitlyn Lamping

cerns, but these visits are intended to prevent health problems, rather than treat them. Catching serious health conditions in their early stages can potentially save your dog's life. Additionally, routine veterinary appointments give you the chance to discuss your dog's weight and overall health with your veterinarian. You'll also be able to keep her up to date on vaccinations and deworming.

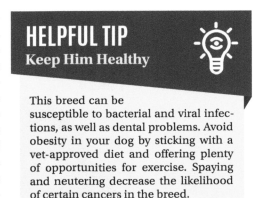

HELPFUL TIP
Keep Him Healthy

This breed can be susceptible to bacterial and viral infections, as well as dental problems. Avoid obesity in your dog by sticking with a vet-approved diet and offering plenty of opportunities for exercise. Spaying and neutering decrease the likelihood of certain cancers in the breed.

Fleas and Ticks

Keeping your dog free from external parasites is not only important for your Ridgeback's health, but for your human family as well. Fleas and ticks can carry and transmit a variety of diseases to both dogs and humans. Fleas can carry tapeworms as well as bartonella bacteria, which can cause an infection with symptoms similar to Lyme disease. Fleas can also be responsible for a skin condition known as flea allergy dermatitis that can cause your dog's skin to become itchy and inflamed due to an allergic reaction to the fleas' saliva. In cases of severe flea infestations, animals can even become anemic, due to blood loss from the fleas feeding. Ticks are also carriers of diseases such as Rocky Mountain spotted fever, Lyme disease, ehrlichiosis, and babesiosis.

The climate in which you live will determine whether or not your dog needs year-round flea and tick prevention. In warmer climates, there is a higher chance of your dog becoming infected any time of the year, whereas colder climates may reduce the number of months where your dog is at risk. If you board your dog frequently, or take her to doggy daycare, you may need to keep her on flea and tick prevention year-round. Many facilities require all dogs staying with them to receive a treatment prior to their arrival.

Talk to your veterinarian about what product is best for your area and your dog. Most flea and tick prevention, regardless of brand, comes in a plastic vial. To apply, the tip of the vial is broken off and the liquid inside is squeezed out onto the back of your dog's neck, where she cannot lick it off. Although Ridgebacks do not have a long coat, it's important that the liquid come into contact with as much skin as possible, so part the hair before ap-

plying. Some dogs may have an allergic reaction to any brand of flea and tick prevention, so keep a close eye on your Ridgeback the first time you apply it. Symptoms include hives, itching, respiratory distress, vomiting, and diarrhea. Severe reactions may include muscle tremors, incoordination, and even death, so use extreme caution until you know how your dog will respond to flea and tick prevention.

Flea and tick collars are also an option, but are generally not recommended, especially if you have other pets in your home. Some collars contain harsh insecticides, such as tetrachlorvinphos, that can cause severe reactions and can be fatal, especially in cats. Some dogs may also experience serious reactions to flea and tick collars, such as skin irritation, hair loss, gastrointestinal upset, and even seizures. The Environmental Protection Agency also considers tetrachlorvinphos to be a carcinogen, so you may also be inadvertently putting your human family members at risk by using these collars.

Worms and Parasites

Protecting your Rhodesian Ridgeback from internal parasites is just as important as keeping her free from fleas and ticks. Many intestinal parasites can also be passed to humans, so regular deworming is crucial. The type of parasites your dog is at risk of contracting vary by area.

Intestinal worms are especially common in puppies, who generally pick them up from adult dogs in their home, often their mothers. They are passed from one animal to another when an uninfected animal ingests the parasite's eggs or larvae, which are often found in contaminated water, food, soil, or feces. The most common types of worms in dogs are roundworms, hookworms, whipworms, and tapeworms. Worms are not the only type of internal parasite though. Protozoa such as coccidia and giardia can also be ingested by dogs. Depending on the area that you live in, you may also need to watch out for heartworms, which are passed from one dog to another by mosqui-

Photo Courtesy of
Iztok Mozina

tos. Although most intestinal parasite infections are easily treated, heartworm can be riskier, so prevention is key. As the name implies, heartworms live in the heart and bloodstream. During treatment, an infected dog's activity level must be closely monitored so that the dying worms do not travel through the dog's circulatory system too quickly and potentially block vital arteries.

Symptoms of internal parasites include diarrhea, vomiting, weight loss, and anemia. Dogs with a heavy load of parasites may appear malnourished, but with a distended belly. Dogs may also seem lethargic or exhibit a severe cough. However, it should be noted that some dogs may display no symptoms at all, so regular testing and deworming is necessary for detection and prevention.

Detecting internal parasites is a relatively simple procedure. Your veterinarian may take a fecal sample from your dog and examine it under a microscope for any sign of eggs or larvae. To test for heartworm, the veterinarian will need to draw a sample of your dog's blood. The blood sample is then mixed with a chemical solution and placed onto a disposable testing device. The results are usually ready to read after about fifteen minutes. Depending on the parasites found in your dog's blood or fecal samples, either oral medication or injections will be prescribed. Treatment times will range from just a few days to several months.

Holistic Alternatives and Supplements

Holistic veterinary care is rising in popularity as people search for more natural ways to keep their dogs healthy. Holistic medicine involves treating the patient with both conventional and alternative therapies, in whatever combination is necessary to heal them. If needed, patients may be treated with the same modern surgeries and medications found in conventional veterinary medicine. Those treatments may also be combined with therapies such chiropractic adjustments, acupuncture, herbal medicine, and even nutritional therapy.

If your dog is experiencing a medical emergency, traditional veterinary medicine will be the best choice, but for dogs suffering from chronic conditions, alternative therapies may be able to provide some relief. Holistic medicine treats the animal's body as a whole rather than a series of individual parts. For example, if your Ridgeback is suffering from arthritis in her hips, a combination of nutritional changes, acupuncture, or massage may be able to help. Although the source of the pain is in your dog's hips, a holistic veterinarian will focus on improving your dog's overall health in order to treat the specific problem area.

If you're interested in visiting a holistic veterinarian, take a look at the American Holistic Veterinary Medical Association's website. They have a list of approved holistic veterinarians in the United States and Canada that can be searched by the species treated as well as the specific types of treatment offered. Many vets specialize either by species or by treatment, so the search feature can help narrow down your options.

Vaccinations

Photo Courtesy of Stephanie Egger

Regardless of breed or size, all dogs require core vaccinations for the most common diseases. These protect against diseases that are prevalent no matter where you live, such as rabies and parvovirus. Core vaccines typically contain antibodies for several different diseases within a single syringe. The most common vaccine is referred to as DHPP, or a five-way vaccine. DHPP protects against parvovirus, adenovirus cough, distemper, hepatitis, and parainfluenza. You may also have the option of a seven-way vaccine, which also includes leptospirosis and coronavirus. As puppies, most dogs receive a series of three core vaccinations at six, twelve, and sixteen weeks of age. As adults, core vaccines are given either once per year or once every three years. Your vet will be able to give you more information about what is required in your area and how often your dog needs vaccinated.

Rabies is the only core vaccine required by law in the United States. Your Ridgeback will receive his first rabies vaccine at around 16 weeks of age. After that, he will receive them once per year or once every three years. Some areas require dogs to be vaccinated yearly, while others accept them every three years. Your veterinarian will be familiar with your local laws, so if you have any questions, don't hesitate to ask.

Depending on your area and your veterinarian's recommendations, you may also need to give your dog non-core vaccines. Common non-core vaccines include Lyme disease, leptospirosis, kennel cough (Bordetella), and rattlesnake venom. Typically, these do not protect the animal as well or for as long as core vaccines. Many boarding kennels, however, require proof of a kennel cough vaccination before dogs are allowed to stay with them.

Allergic reactions are possible with vaccines, so it's important to keep a close watch on your dog following any vaccinations. If your dog is sensitive to vaccines, you may want to consider only giving her one at a time. You'll need to make several appointments if your dog is due for more than one vaccine, but the extra time is worth it to keep your dog safe. Symptoms of an allergic reaction include swelling of the face or paws, hives, vomiting, lethargy, and pain or swelling at the injection site. Severe reactions may also include difficulty breathing and seizures. If you are unsure about your dog's reactions to vaccines, you may want to wait around at the vet clinic for a few minutes to make sure your dog will handle it well. Serious reactions can be fatal if not treated immediately.

As an alternative to yearly vaccines, many veterinarians offer titer testing. Titer testing measures the antibodies in your Ridgeback's blood. If the levels are high enough and your local laws allow it, your dog won't need to be vaccinated. Titer testing only works with core vaccines, as non-core vaccines do not last long enough to be tested for. Typically, your vet will draw a small blood sample and either test the blood at the clinic, or send it off to a laboratory for testing. Titer testing can be more expensive than regular vaccines, but if your dog is sensitive to vaccines, it may be your best option.

Pet Insurance

To keep up with the rising costs of veterinary care, many owners have turned to pet insurance to help cover their dog's medical expenses. There are many different companies that offer a variety of plans for different budgets. You can choose your plan based on the amount of coverage as well as the monthly premium. As with human health insurance, preexisting conditions are rarely covered, and some pets may require higher monthly premiums or even be denied coverage based on their current health or age. Unfortunately, most pet insurance plans do not cover the cost of routine preventative care. Regular exams, vaccinations, and dental care will likely need to be paid for out-of-pocket.

Some people claim that they will never own a dog without insuring her, while others think the idea is frivolous, especially for dogs who are healthy and remain accident free for many years. Avid supporters claim that in costly emergency situations, their plans have saved them thousands of dollars. Those monthly premiums can add up quickly and many pet owners instead choose to set aside a small amount of money each month in case of emergencies. It's important to do plenty of research with a few different insurance companies before deciding whether pet insurance is right for you and your dog.

CHAPTER 17
Advanced Rhodesian Ridgeback Health and Aging Dog Care

Common Diseases and Conditions in Rhodesian Ridgebacks

Hip dysplasia is most commonly found in larger breeds such as the Rhodesian Ridgeback. The condition is due to an abnormally developed hip joint, which results in the breakdown of cartilage. This deterioration will lead to severe arthritis and pain, though each dog may react differently. Symptoms of hip dysplasia can include decreased activity level and range of motion, as well as limping or swaying during normal movements. Nearly three-quarters of dogs with hip dysplasia are able to live happy and functional lives, but proper lifestyle management is key. Weight control and physical exercise are essential to keeping dysplastic dogs healthy and fit.

Photo Courtesy of Linda Hafer

Pain management medication and surgery are also possible treatments in more severe cases.

Similar to hip dysplasia, elbow dysplasia is a condition caused by an abnormality in the elbow joint. However, the term 'elbow dysplasia' actually covers a variety of specific conditions including osteochondrosis (OCD), fragmented coronoid process (FCP), and joint incongruity, to name just a few. Elbow dysplasia can be genetic, or it can be a result of an injury or dietary deficiency. It is also most commonly diagnosed in large and giant breeds. The condition can be detected in dogs as young as five months of age, but diagnosis after the age of four is more common. Symptoms include an asymmetrical gait, limping, and a decrease in activity. Treatment will vary depending on the specific cause of the disease, but often surgical intervention is necessary.

Autoimmune thyroiditis is another condition often found in Rhodesian Ridgebacks, but luckily it is not life-threatening. The disease causes hypothyroidism, which is when the thyroid gland does not make enough thyroxine. Thyroxine is a hormone that controls the dog's metabolism. Most dogs begin to develop symptoms between two and five years of age. Symptoms of hypothyroidism include weight gain or obesity, hair loss, and skin issues. Autoimmune thyroiditis is easily detectable with a simple blood test. It can even be detected before a dog begins to show symptoms, so regular testing is recommended if you believe your dog is at risk. Treatment is usually inexpensive and consists of a daily supplement or medication.

Genetic Traits Found in Rhodesian Ridgebacks

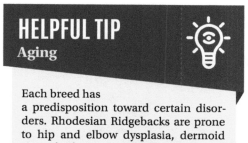

HELPFUL TIP

Aging

Each breed has a predisposition toward certain disorders. Rhodesian Ridgebacks are prone to hip and elbow dysplasia, dermoid sinus (DS), neural tube defects in the back, neck, and tail, as well as bloat. Bloat is a life-threatening condition dog owners should be prepared for in their large dogs. Consult your veterinarian about signs, symptoms, and what to do if this happens to your dog. Be prepared.

Congenital deafness does not occur frequently in Rhodesian Ridgebacks, but it is a known problem with the breed. Although it sometimes occurs due to conditions experienced while in the womb, such as intrauterine infections or toxin exposures, it's more often inherited. Inherited deafness is usually caused by a gene defect, but it's nearly impossible to determine the cause of deafness unless it has been noted in previous generations. Breeders can test puppies for deafness after 35 days of age using the Brainstem Auditory Evoked Response, or BAER, test. This test uses earphones to send auditory signals to the dog, whose responses are then recorded. Dogs who are found to be deaf in one or both ears are then eliminated from the breeding pool by spaying or neutering.

Rhodesian Ridgeback Inherited Arrythmia, or RRIVA, is a cardiac disease that puppies can inherit from their parents. It is an abnormality in the heart's electrical system, which leads to irregular heartbeats. In extreme cases, this condition can be fatal. Most dogs exhibit the most severe symptoms between 6 and 30 months of age, though some actually outgrow the issue. Thankfully, the mutated genes associated with the disease can be detected using a DNA test. This allows breeders to make responsible decisions regarding which dogs they should and should not breed, to help reduce the prevalence of the condition within the breed.

Basics of Senior Dog Care

Large breeds such as Rhodesian Ridgebacks are typically considered to be senior dogs at around seven years of age. This does not mean you need to make serious changes to your dog's lifestyle the day she turns seven, it simply means that you can expect to see changes in your dog's physical abilities and personality at around that age. Aging affects each dog differently so some dogs may start acting older when they are younger than

Photo Courtesy of
Gail Krenn

seven, and other may not show any signs of old age until they are closer to ten years old. Certain health conditions may also cause some dogs to age prematurely.

As your Ridgeback ages, you may begin to notice changes in both her behavior and his body. Long walks may become shorter, and her play sessions may become less rambunctious. Older dogs tend to sleep more and may be a bit stiff getting out of bed in the mornings. Some senior dogs may experience hearing loss or impaired sight, so you may need to be more cautious when approaching your dog from behind or waking her from naps. You might also notice that your Ridgeback needs to go outside more frequently, or she may begin to have accidents in the house. It's common for senior dogs to suffer from incontinence. It's also possible for dogs to begin to develop symptoms of cognitive dysfunction, also known as dementia. Dogs with dementia may seem confused at times, or they may become more fearful or aggressive. No matter what signs of aging your dog displays, it's important to take notice and adjust your dog's care and environment accordingly.

Grooming

As your Rhodesian Ridgeback ages, his grooming needs may change. Whether you groom your Ridgeback yourself or have a professional take care of it, it's important that you stick to a normal grooming routine. The time spent grooming your dog is an opportunity for you or your groomer to check the overall health of his skin and coat. As dogs age, sometimes their hair begins to thin or they develop various lumps and bumps. Grooming gives you the opportunity to keep a close eye on any problems or potential problems. You'll be able to check your dog over in a way that you probably wouldn't with just petting or showing her affection.

In addition to changes in the coat and skin, standing for long periods of time while being bathed or brushed may become difficult or even impossible for your Ridgeback. Because of this, many groomers choose to groom senior dogs in a series of short sessions, allowing them to rest for 15-20 minutes between each session. Dogs developing symptoms of dementia may become more difficult to work with. Groomers will also need to be more cautious about handling your senior Ridgeback due to arthritic joints and delicate skin.

Nutrition

It's not uncommon for older dogs to begin to gain weight as they slow down, so you may need to adjust your Ridgeback's diet. Although many older dogs gain weight, there are many that have a difficult time keeping weight on and may become rather thin. That said, obesity is a common condition among senior dogs and care must be taken to avoid it as extra weight puts more strain on arthritic joints, which can further affect mobility.

As your Ridgeback ages and his overall health changes, you may need to adjust his diet to accommodate any health conditions that he may develop. Dogs suffering from diabetes or heart disease will need a special type of food. Many specialized diets like this must be prescribed by a veterinarian and can only be purchased at a veterinary clinic.

Owners of senior Rhodesian Ridgebacks often choose to supplement their dog's diet, rather than making significant changes. Joint supplements such as glucosamine, chondroitin sulfate, and hyaluronic acid can help ease the pain of arthritis. You may also consider adding a fiber supplement or probiotics to your aging dog's diet to ease age-related gastrointestinal distress. Some older dogs may lose their appetites, so you might need to consider adding appealing toppers to your Ridgeback's food. Bone broth, canned food, or even warm water can help make a meal more appetizing. Before you begin adding any supplements to your dog's diet, discuss your dog's current health and diet with your vet.

Exercise

As your Rhodesian Ridgeback's metabolism slows and his joints begin to ache more, even the most rambunctious dog will begin to slow down. The exact age at which this occurs will vary, but certain chronic conditions may limit your dog's mobility earlier than expected. Exercise becomes increasingly important as dogs age in order to prevent weight gain, which can cause further joint damage and pain. However, senior dogs should not be forced to exercise any more than they are comfortable with, as this can lead to more pain and potentially injury.

Regardless of what age your Ridgeback begins to slow down, it's important to maintain a safe environment for your dog to exercise in. Long flights of stairs and slick floors can be dangerous for older dogs, so if you exercise your dog indoors, make sure you do so on carpeted floors without too many obstacles. If you would prefer to work with your dog outside, grass is a great surface for older dogs as it provides an appropriate amount of grip and cushion. As physical exertion becomes more difficult, you may want to offer your aging dog more mental stimulation. It's common for older dogs' bodies to slow down before their minds, so mental stimulation can be a great way to keep them busy without the discomfort associated with physical activity.

Common Old-age Ailments

Arthritis is one of the most common conditions found in aging Rhodesian Ridgebacks. They may develop arthritis in any part of their body, but it's most common in hips, knees, elbows, and the back. It's also common for aging Ridgebacks to lose their sight or hearing, so you may need to be more careful, so you don't startle your dog. Older dogs may want to sleep for longer periods, and they may only be interested in short walks or play sessions. As your Ridgeback begins to exhibit more signs of old age, it's essential that you make the necessary changes to his lifestyle and environment to accommodate his changing needs. Older dogs often need to go outside more often, and you may need to adjust his diet more than once. Some dogs can be somewhat difficult to manage in their older years, due to changes in health or behavior, but it's important to reflect on all of the joy you've shared throughout your time together.

When It's Time to Say Goodbye

It is heartbreaking to say goodbye to your beloved Rhodesian Ridgeback, but the time will come for every dog. You must be thankful for all of the happiness she has given you and remember all of the good times you've had with your best friend. This may be a time for mourning, but it's also an opportunity to celebrate your dog's life and the adventures you've had together.

As your dog's final hours approach, it may be difficult to make the necessary arrangements, but your veterinarian will be able to guide you through the process. Many vets offer euthanasia services both in-clinic as well as in your home. Some owners may find it difficult to say goodbye in the public setting of a veterinary clinic, so in-home services are best. Others may not want to have the memory of the end taking place in their home. Whichever you find more comforting, you will be able to find a supportive veterinary team to help you through this trying time. As long as you are there for your Ridgeback, he will be comforted knowing that his final moments were spent with his beloved family.

Lightning Source UK Ltd.
Milton Keynes UK
UKHW020625240122
397613UK00001B/7

9 781952 069291